How To Sew Art

volume 2.0

Learn To Easily Transform Ordinary Fabric Into Family Treasures

Tammie Bowser

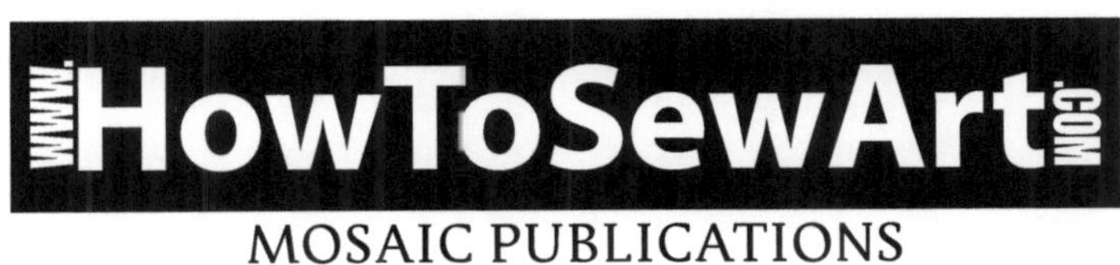

MOSAIC PUBLICATIONS

Author: Tammie Bowser
Editor: Denise Roberson
Book Design & Illustrations: Tammie Bowser

All quilts designed and made by Tammie Bowser except where indicated

Library of Congress Cataloging in Publication Data
Bowser, Tammie
How To Sew Art volume 2/ Tammie Bowser
ISBN 1-887467-04-1 (paper trade)
1. Quilting. 2. Quilting -- Art.
3. Quilting--Applique.
1. Title.

Library of Congress Control Number: 2017904491

Published by:

Mosaic Publications
South Pasadena, California 91031

Printed in the U.S.A.

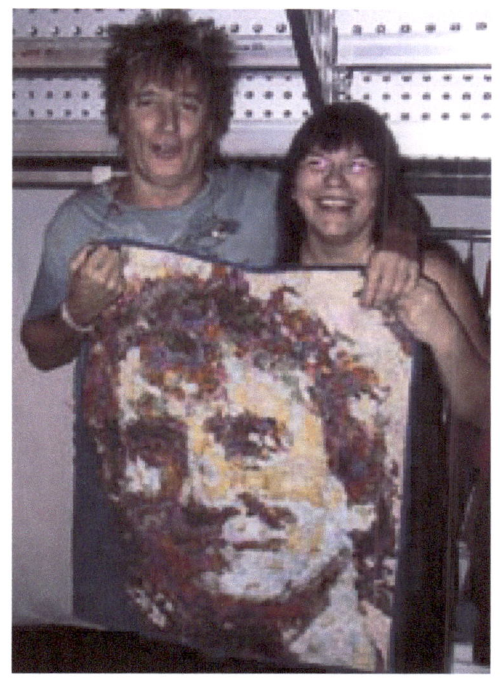

Hi Tammie,
Well, I finally finished my Rod Stewart wall hanging just in time for Rod's current tour. I was undecided whether to give it to him or not but I took it to the Vancouver concert to show it to him during the concert. The end result being that we went to his dressing room and I got to show it to him and he loved it. He said that we was going to get it framed, so needless to say I gave him the wall hanging and have a picture with him and the wall hanging. I also got a hug and 3 kissesfor my efforts.I really enjoyed doing the quilted photo and will have to do another one of Rod so that I can keep it. Everybody justs loves the results and are amazed that it is made of fabric.

Thanks again for showing me a wonderful way to reproduce my pictures using fabrics.
Thanks
Jean Allbeury

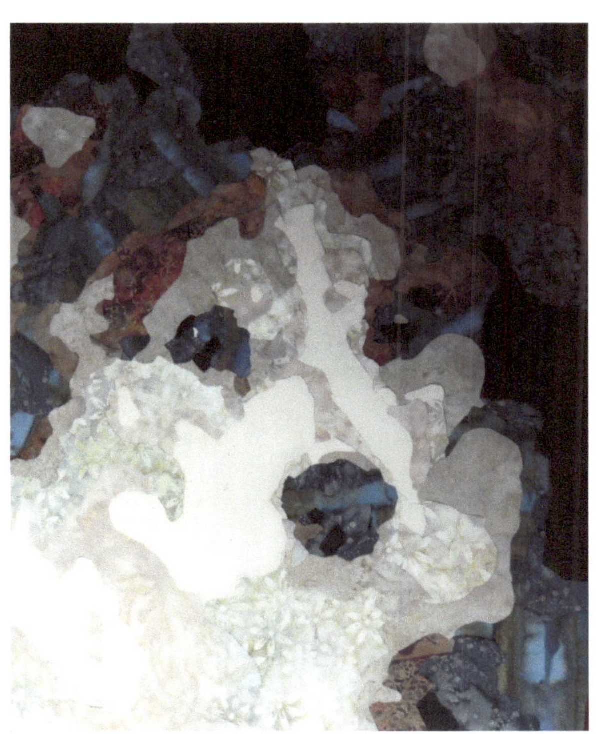

It was a fun class!
Hi Tammie, My name is Anne Gavin and I wanted to show you the piece I finished from your class at Hampton Roads in February. It was a fun class and I enjoyed it so much. Thanks for all your help.
Anne Gavin

We enjoyed your class very much. You made it so easy. We had so many great comments on the quilts we made. We are planning on making 6 more!
Martha Christensen & Cora Hall
Carson, CA

Dear Tammie,
I am thankful that your class was available. After ten years, it took my quilting to a higher level!
Ozellia Crawford
Los Angeles, CA

Quilted Photography is totally unique and exciting. It involves two things that makes me love quilting, it's looks hard but is really quite simple. And it is fun too!
Jan Emanuel
Pasadena, CA

I learned more about color value in the one day class than at Art School! Tammie's instructions were great! I watched my photo come to life in the class. I will treasure my quilt for a lifetime!
Darlen Lee
Acton, CA

I learned so much about the color value of fabrics! I now use this knowledge on other quilt blocks and wearable art. What a valuable addition to my quilting education!
Thank You
Annette Berry
Los Angeles, CA

Tammie's method is ingenious! I was able to make a beautiful mosaic quilt in color from a black and white photo of my mother as a child from 1937. I created an heirloom quilt that will be in the family for generations to come. The technique is so simple even a novice quilter can create an incredible piece of textile art. I am currently working on another portrait, and plan to make quilts of more family members, this is addictive!
Thanks Tammie!

Cheryll Handy
Pasadena, CA

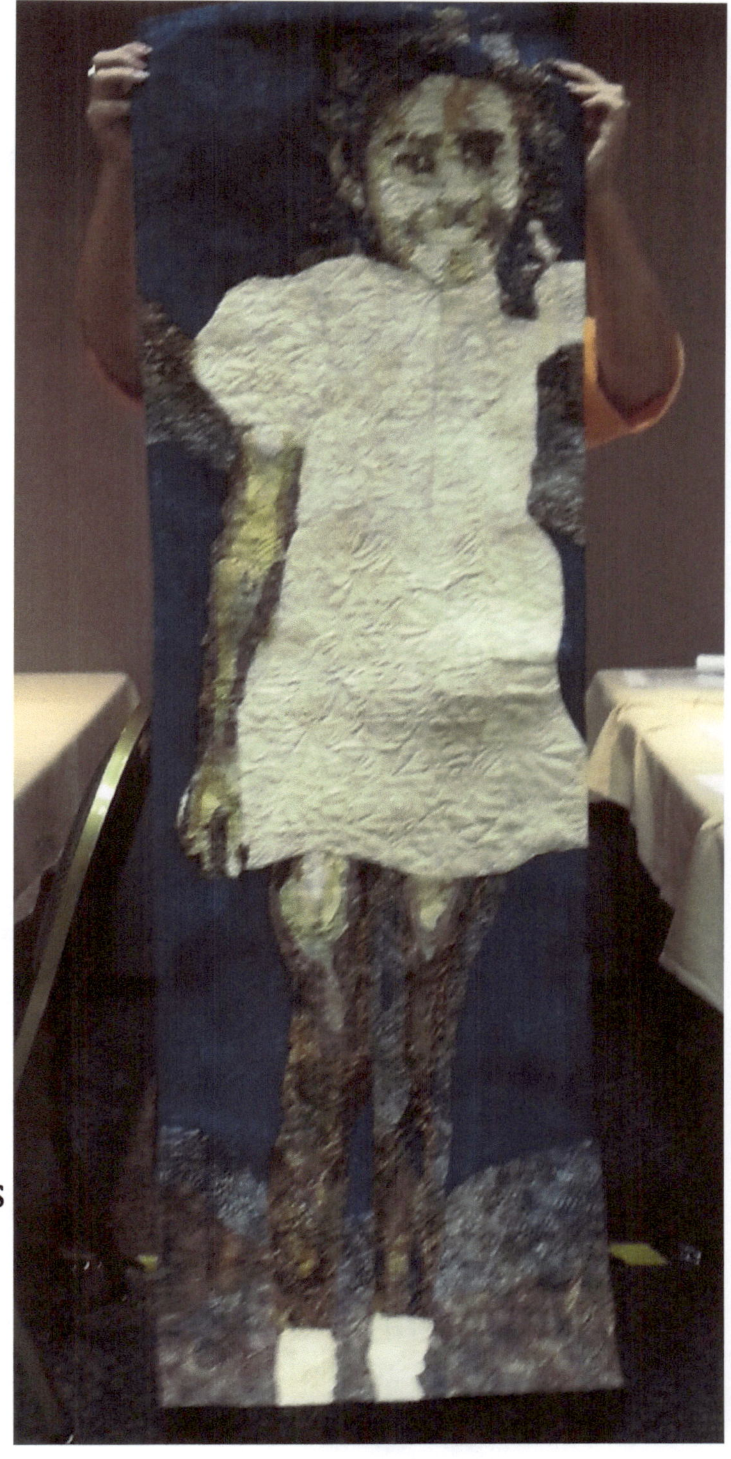

"Tammie Bowser's methods give you the tools to make heirloom-quality quilts on your first try. She has created a program that breaks down a process that would be unfathomably complicated for a busy quilter and makes it fun and fast to do. The results are nothing short of stunning in every case."

Sue Ann Taylor
Founder of Quilters News Network

"Your favorite photos recreated in fabric... what a fabulous idea! Tammie's easy to follow directions and her color value theories will help you preserve a memory in fabric"...

Kaye Wood
Television show host and author of 28 quilting books

Quilted Photography is just fabulous! Creating a quilt with your cherished photo on it is a great idea. My daughter Rosie (16 years old) and I have enjoyed making your quilts. It is something we enjoy doing together.
Kath Robi
Pasadena, CA

It was a fun experience to watch my photo "appear" as the fabric pieces were added!
Marcy Young
Sherman Oaks, CA

Tammie is a lovely, energetic & wildly creative woman! I thought quilted photography would be intense and difficult, but with amazing results only half of that is true, her technique is simple, clear and it does yield amazing results!
Alexis Durham
Manhattan Beach, CA

For a long time I had been trying to introduce pictures into my quilts, so I learned different techniques to make memory quilts. It was OK for a while, but your Quilted Photography was what I was looking for! It is a real picture experience. I LOVE IT!
Francisca Reynoso
Valley Glen, CA

I Loved your class. I did a combination of my 2 grandchildren. Everyone loves it. I had a lot of enjoyment working on it.

Jo Ann Felter
Buena Park, CA

These quilts are extremely easy and fun to make! They make great gift quilts. The instructions are easy to follow and your class was a lot of fun! This is a great quilt for any beginner or advanced quilter!

Sue Vite

I found the Mosaic Quilt Studio on the web and was simply floored by the images and possibilities. The class was fantastic and I continue to work on photo quilts. The quilt I made in class has won "First Place" in two shows, one "Judges Choice" and one "Best of Show"!

Marlene Pearson
Santa Barbara, CA

Thank you for inspiring me to make mosaic fabric photographs of everyone in my family for Christmas presents this year (2003). I began in January and by 11:30pm December 24th, I had finished eighteen! When I saw episode #819 of Simply Quilts, I called you on the phone and you were kind enough to spend quite a while encouraging me. Thanks again!

Peggy Johnson
Lake Oswego, OR

I certainly like the results of my taking your class. The ease of picking the colors and swatches to develop the picture was phenomenal! The class was well taught!

Sara Brandon
Los Angeles, CA

Making my mosaic quilt was fast, fun & easy. Not at all as hard as it looks. Everyone that sees my quilt is impressed, especially my six year old son (he is on the quilt). I can't believe I made it in one class. Can't wait to make my other two kids a picture quilt!

Debbie Hoshizaki
Los Angeles, CA

My quilt turned out beautifully - I didn't realize that my cat was ill when I started working on it. As I neared the end, he being quite ill, he sat with me as I finished the quilt. He died as I finished the quilt. I was able to have him near as our time together ended... The quilt sits above the piano now.

Ingrid Margolin
Glendale, CA

I've been quilting for 3 years and have never seen anything like your quilts, and I just had to take your class! It looked difficult but in fact is so easy and fun!! It was like paint by number but with fabric. Thanks for bringing this technique to us.

Debbie Sparr
Los Angeles, CA

"Tammie's quilted photos are so slick to make; they come together like magic! Besides being fun to make, It's fun to bask in all the compliments."
Ami Simms
Quilt book author, award winning quilter

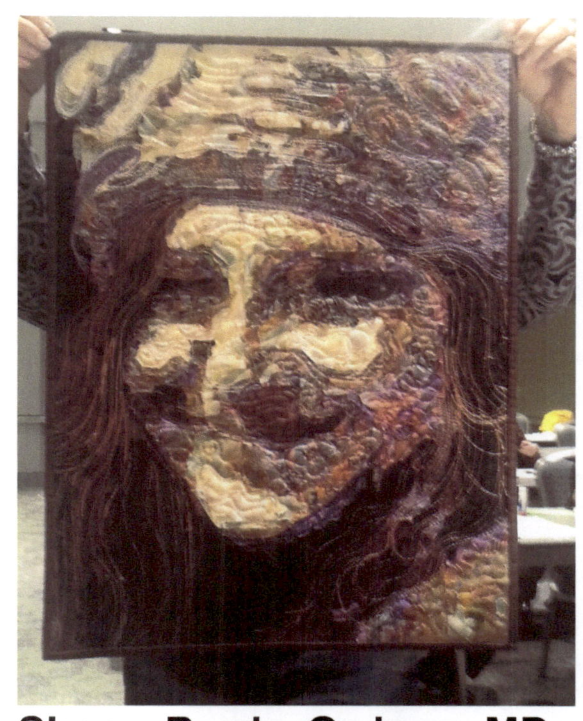

Sherry Brady, Owings, MD

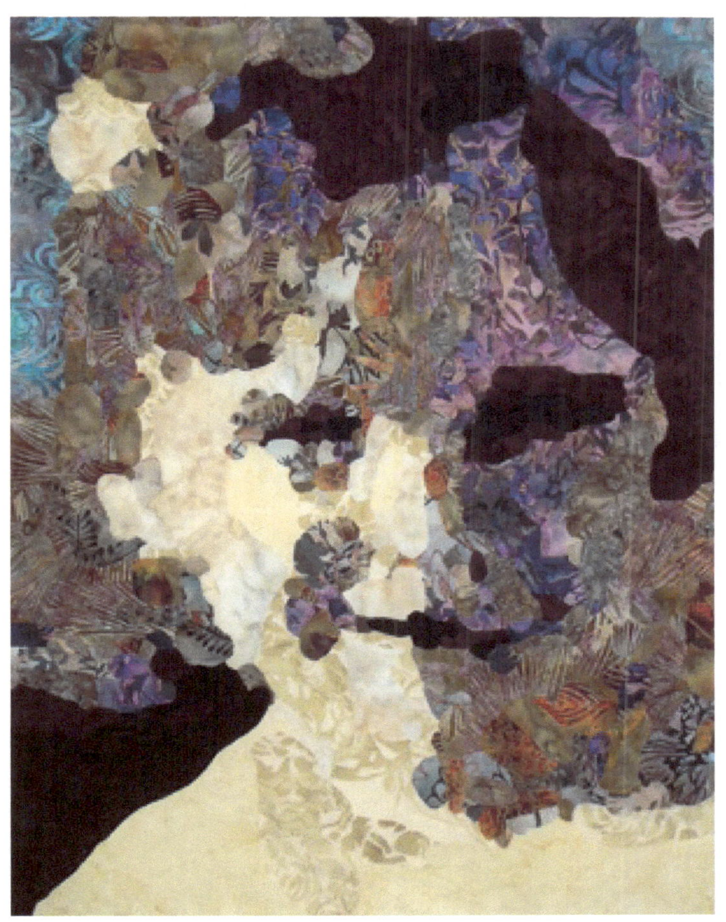

I had a great time making "Evan" my grandson. At first I thought this is not looking like anything and "pow" there he was. This work has won 2 awards. One for a quilt show and one for an art show. So exciting!

Thank you
Pat Carlson

PS Tammie your process is fun and exciting to do.

Tammie, Through you I have really found my artistic voice. I met you in Nashville and my art life has never been the same. This is an awesome technique! I LOVE IT!!!

Lisa Bova

Tammie, I really enjoyed making this quilt — it was such fun to see my husband come to life before my eyes! I made the quilt for a challenge project in our quilt guild. The theme was "When Quilters Talk, They Say It With Color." Blue is associated with depth and stability. It symbolizes trust, loyalty, wisdom,confidence, intelligence, understanding, integrity, seriousness, and truth — all attributes that describe my husband. The technique used to make the quilt also represents Al's ability to move beyond the minute details in order to see the big picture of any situation. He is my true blue love, so I named the quilt, My True Blue You/Love Is Blue. Thanks for providing a terrific computer program that helped make this quilt so much fun to make!

Annie Unrein

Tammie, I wanted to share my first quilt with you. I have been thinking about making a quilt for several years, but didn't feel I had the time. When I saw you on Sewing with Nancy, I immediately looked for your website as I knew that this process would be relatively quick. I loved pressing the pieces on and seeing the pattern come to life. Thanks for your software and your quilting process. I have attached both my quilt and the photo I used for the pattern.

Regards,

Shari Sands

"These quilts are extremely easy and fun to make! They make great gift quilts. The instructions are easy to follow and your class was a lot of fun! This is a great quilt for any beginner or advanced quilter!"

Sue Vite

Table Of Contents

A Note To The Reader

Thank you to all of my past students, for inspiring me and sharing your photos and comments with me.

Most of all, I want to thank The Most High God Of Everything for this endless source of creative ideas.

Before we get into the lessons, I want you to remember that this technique was designed specifically to take a DRAWING or PAINTING and make it into fabric art. That means a photo or a photographic picture is not suitable for this technique. If you want to do a photographic picture, use my other technique in "How To Sew Art," the first book.

This book has several new ideas that I hope you will ENJOY!

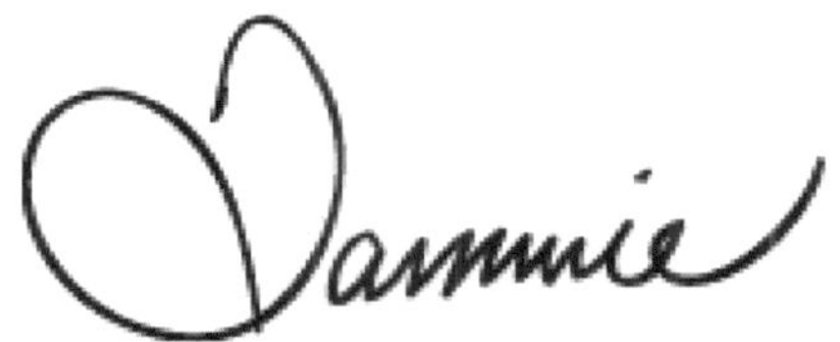

Introduction

If you have a young child or grandchild, you know that with just a piece of paper and a hand full of crayons they can make beautiful pictures.

Children are natural artists and some of those little pictures need to be preserved and highlighted because they are brilliant!

In this book, I'll teach you how to transform those little pictures into treasured art made out of fabric or a giant comfy art quilt for their bed!

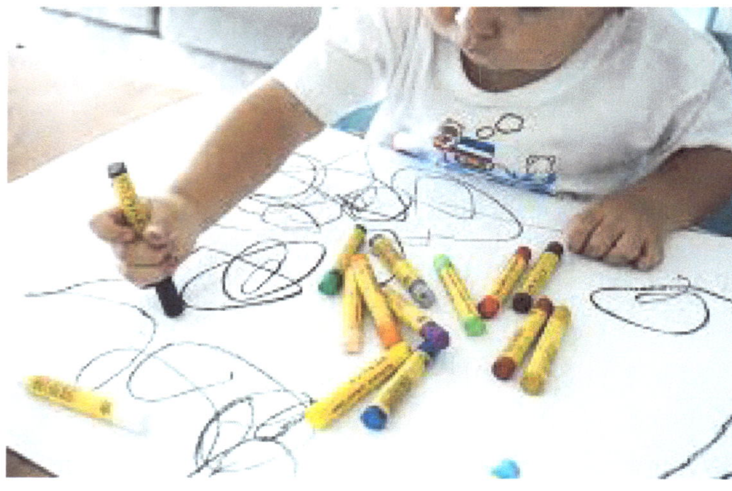

You'll learn this new Quilted Photography™ technique to quickly recreate drawings or paintings as "Stitched Art". In this book, I have decided to focus on children's drawings, but this technique is also great for drawings and paintings made by teens and adults as well!

You'll learn how to use fabric just like it is paint (or crayons / colored pencils)! It is possible and it is also easy if you take time to understand the concepts.

I have a question for you... Do you know what color value is?

ANSWER - Color value is how light or dark a fabric is in relation to the other fabrics around it.

All of my other Quilted Photography™ techniques rely on color value to form the main fabric selections, but for this technique we will use COLOR to recreate the picture. We will use color value only to determine the background.

Even though we will be using color value for selecting the background only, determining the color value of your fabric is one of the most valuable all around quilting skills you can have.

I have found that it is hard for most students to recognize the color value of fabrics. To solve this problem, I have prepared a short video lesson that will teach you 3 ways to easiy recognize the values of your fabrics:

http://HowToSewArt.com/free-value-tool/

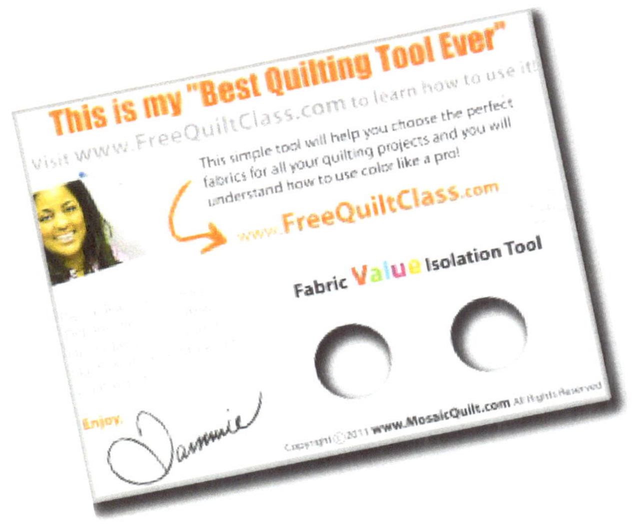

Now lets talk about color and how you can use it to create your drawing/painting. I sometimes like to alter the colors of my images to make an artistic statement, but for this technique I want to stay true to the original colors of the drawing/painting.

Choosing the fabric colors for this technique is simple. You use the colors you see in the drawing!

If your picture has only a few colors, it will be easier than if it has lots of colors.

TIP - Use 6 to 8 colors (or less) and your drawing will be easy to recreate!

To make sure your child/grand child gives you an appropriate picture, only give them a few crayons to draw with!

When you are planning a new project, you also need to focus on the colors you use because people are influenced by colors before anything else.

Here is a list of colors and what they illustrate:

Brown and other earthy tones convey comfort, simplicity, and credibility.

Blue conveys longevity and security. Research shows that blue brings a calming effect and suppresses appetite. Men usually love blue.

Vibrant Red represents high energy and vitality. Red also commands attention. It is exciting and passionate. Women are inclined to like red. Warning: Red is strong and can dominate a color palette.

Orange is friendly and playful. It is casual and full of energy. This hue will certainly demand the viewer's attention.

Yellow is welcoming. It will surely uplift one's energy. It feels warm and cheerful. It is very effective and beautiful when placed beside a dark background.

Green is representative of comfort, health, and growth. It is calming and restful to the eyes.

Black is a powerful and formal color and it can show high style.

Grey is safe, reliable, mature, and somewhat predictable. Grey is also used to give a modern look to your image.

White is simple, clean, attractive, and precise.

TIP - Use color wisely to purposefully choose the kind of impact you intend to make.

Chapter 1

New Ideas

First of all, I want to tell you how this technique is different than my other methods. After I tell you about the new ideas, I'm going to explain each idea so you will understand how to apply the idea in your projects.

New Idea # 1
The art is different for this book. For my previous quilting techniques, I've always used pixels and a camera to create a photograph...but now we are going to use drawings. Drawings can be so cute, especially if you use a drawing from a child or a grandchild. They have lovely meanings and memories associated with them.

This technique allows you to be the artist in a different kind of way. Your child's scribbles and doodles can now be memorialized in fabric. You can use a little hand scribble or you can use a painting.

The snowman picture below is a good example of a type of painting that will work. What's interesting about this painting is that it has a small number of colors and the shapes are simple, but at the same time the picture is still interesting to look at.

New Idea # 2
The picture is very different. You're going to look for different things and learn to pay attention to the complexity of the picture versus the simplicity of the picture.

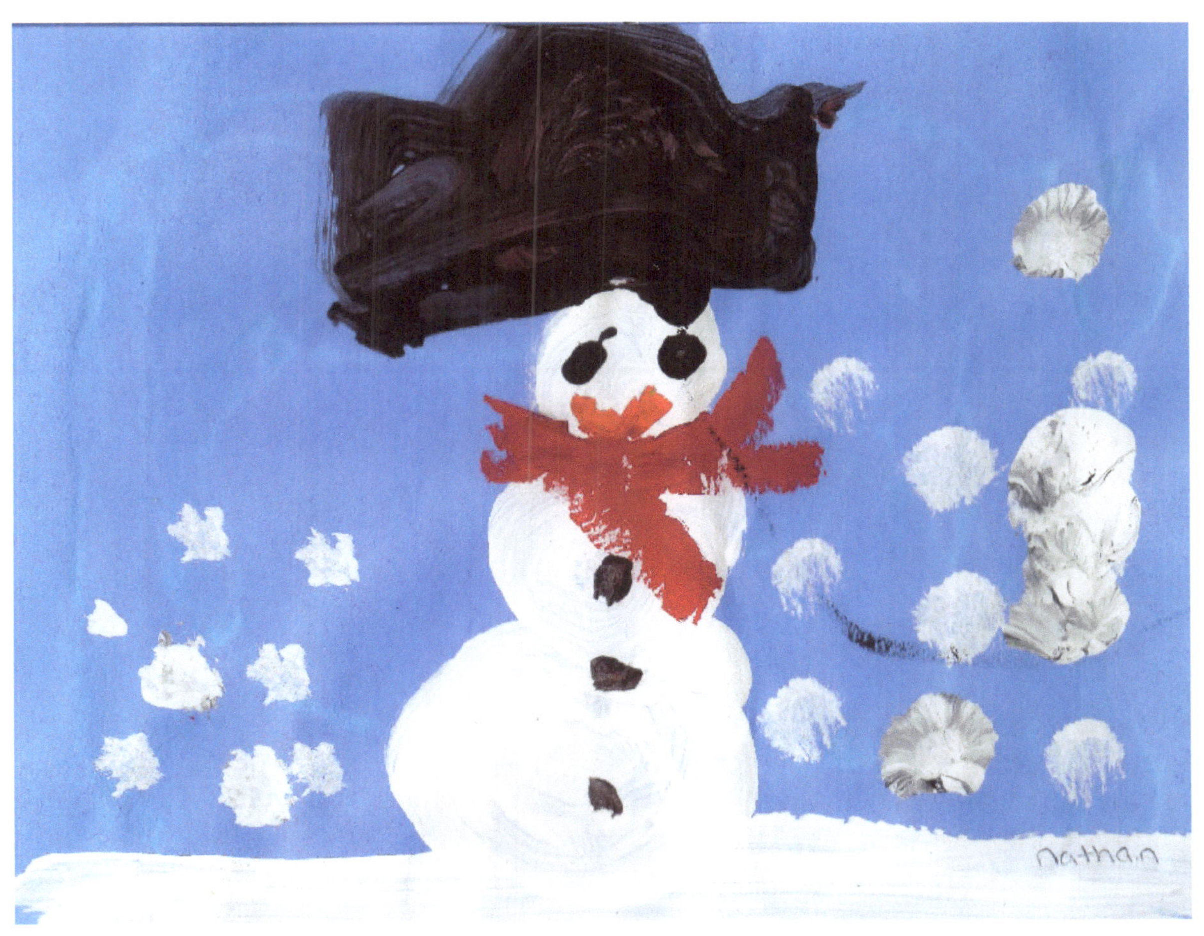

This picture (Exhibit B) appears to be a simple drawing, and it is. However, there is a problem that makes it complicated! It is too complicated because it's really 6 drawings, and that's what makes it unsuitable for this technique.

A student brought this picture (Exhibit B) to class and she was overwhelmed at the amount of work that would be required to make 6 drawings. So I urge you to choose a drawing with one big focus instead of many small focuses. Remember that we want to choose simplicity and we want to avoid complexity.

Now, lets explore the types of pictures to avoid. There are a few rules that must be considered while choosing a picture:

TIP - Avoid complicated pictures or pictures with many elements in them.

Exhibit A

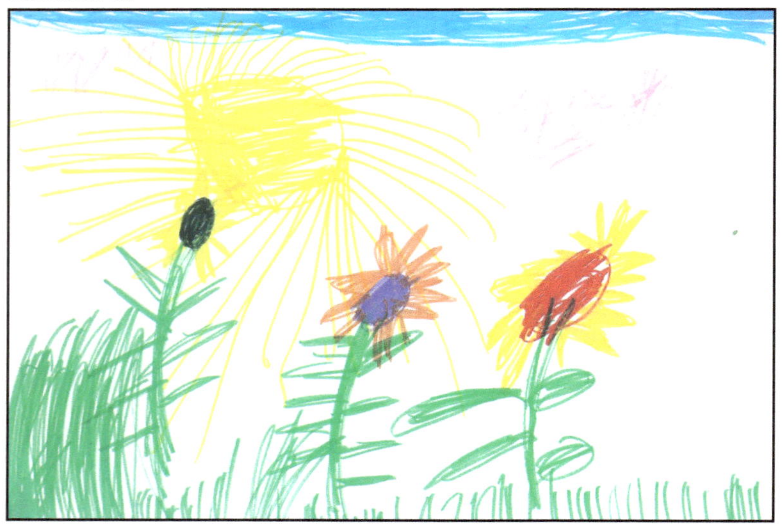

Exhibit A is a very nice picture, but it would be much better with one central focus. You can still use this picture if you crop out some of the elements.

Exhibit B

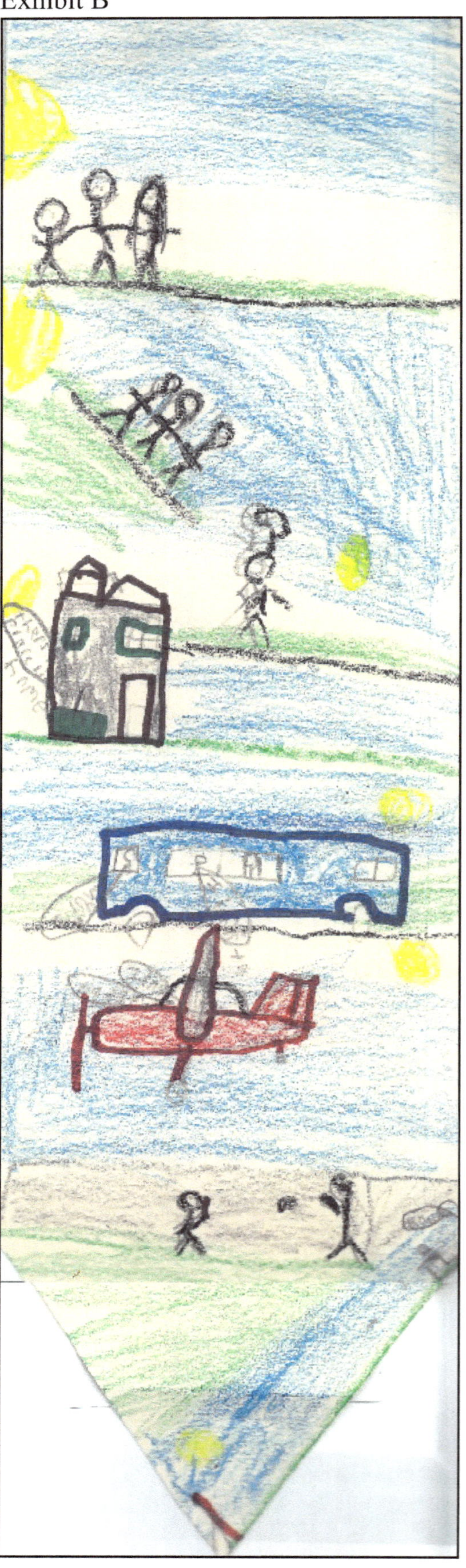

Exhibit C is an example of how you can crop out some of the elements of the same picture to create a better focus. I have kept the sunshine and one flower.

New Idea # 3

Choosing color is different. With my other techniques, we've always relied on color value, but for this technique, we will focus only on color for the main picture.

Exhibit C

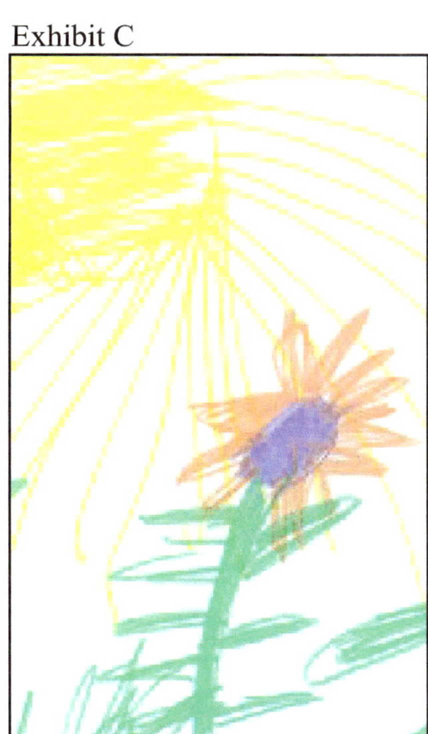

For previous techniques we always started with fabric from light to dark ranging all the way up from white to black, but now we're actually going to pay attention to color. That's why, if you remember to avoid anything complicated, you'll want only a few colors.

TIP - Avoid pictures with many, many colors. If your picture has a complicated mix of colors it will be difficult to choose so many fabrics that work well with one another.

A tip on how to minimize the colors (if you're going to have a grandchild or a child make a drawing) is, don't give them the whole box of crayons. Give them a piece of paper and four to six crayons and let them make something beautiful with just a few colors. Exhibit D was done by a young man

Exhibit D

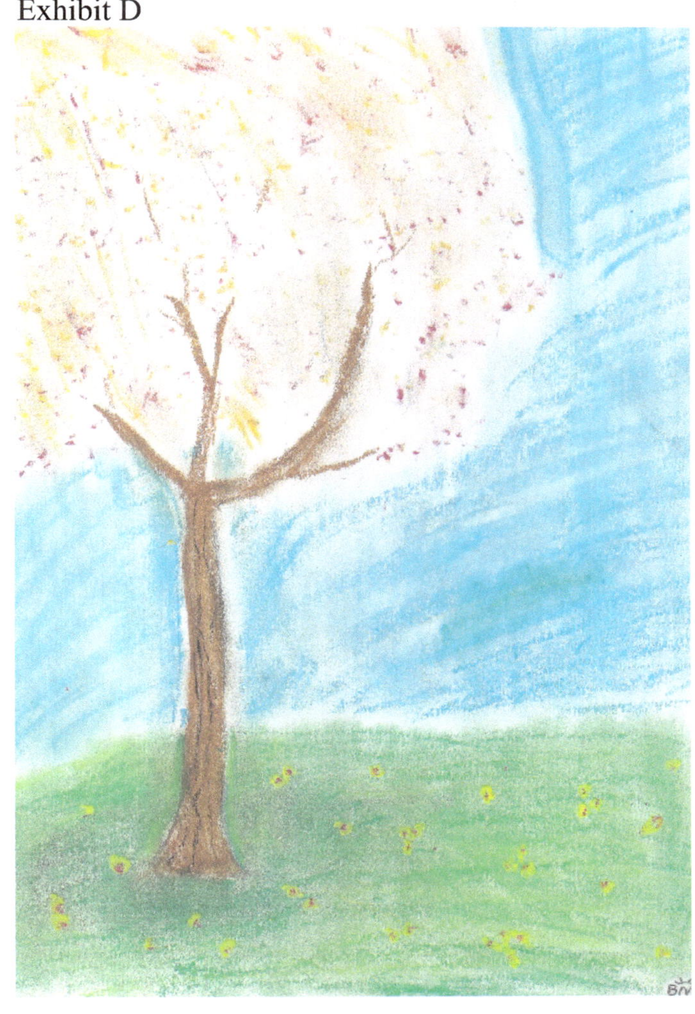

in Arizona. His grandmother came to take my class and I loved the quilt so much that I chose it for the cover of this book! I think it's amazing. It's a perfect example for choosing color, it's a perfect example for the simplicity and it's a perfect example of a simple drawing.

New Idea #4

The stitching is different. For the stitching in my previous techniques, we always use some sort of graphic, or repeating, geometric kind of shape. Some people liked to use what they call meandering or something like that, but again, it was some sort of repeating shape.

But in contrast, what we're going to do is show you how to follow the crayon lines as a guide for how to stitch the quilt. The quilt I made of the drawing below is a good example of this style of stitching. I will go into detail in the "Finishing" chapter on page 77 and you can see the stitched quilt on page 55. The objective was to stitch the quilt following the crayon lines just as the little girl drew them. Following the guide of the drawing lines just as the artist made them is very important for this technique.

Now I want to show you how to make the patterns for this kind of quilt. The best way is to use **"Quilted Photo Deluxe"** software.

Exhibit E

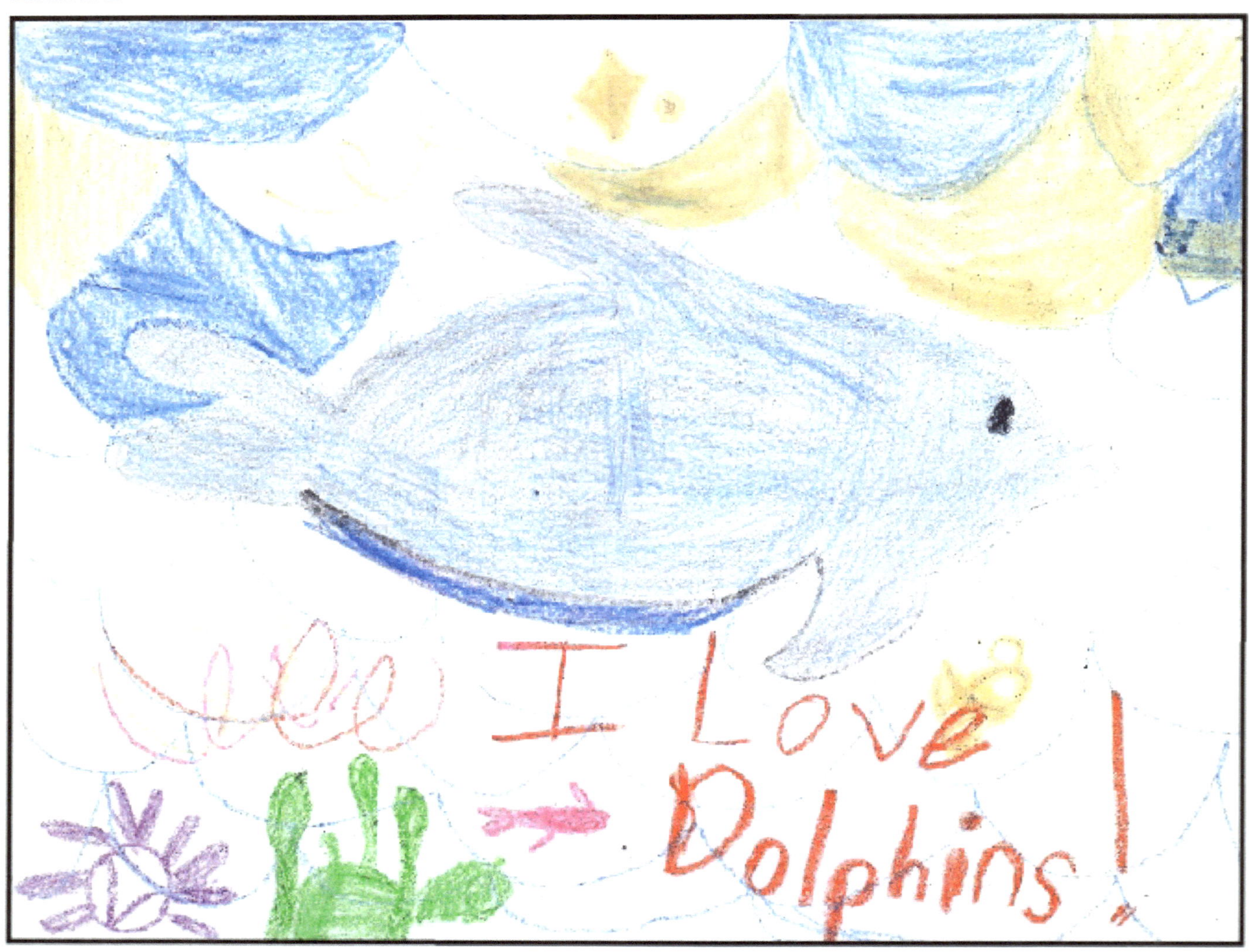

If you don't have the software, you can try out the fully functioning software free for seven full days. I have provided the free trial so that you can make your own patterns. See page 88 for instruction on how to get your free online video course and trial software.

How To Make Pattern

1. The first thing you're going to do is push "New Project" and it will clear the screen so you can start a new project.

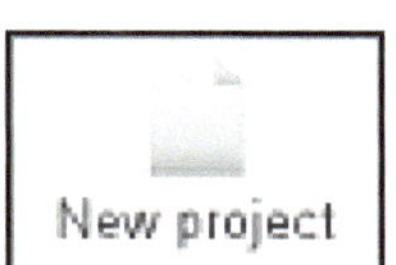

2. Then push "Import Photo" and navigate to where you have your pictures scanned and saved. The picture must be in JPEG format.

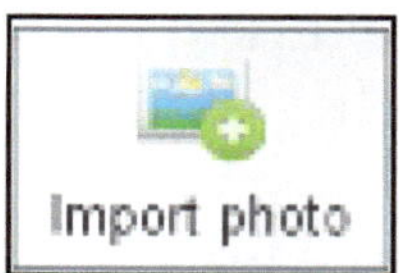

I have chosen this painted picture of little hands (Exhibit F). It's like a finger painting. This is another good option for a type of picture you can choose. These little hands were made with one color of paint, but that doesn't mean you have to choose only one fabric. There's red for the hands and there's beige for the background. I suggest that you choose several beige fabrics for the background and that will make the quilt

Exhibit F

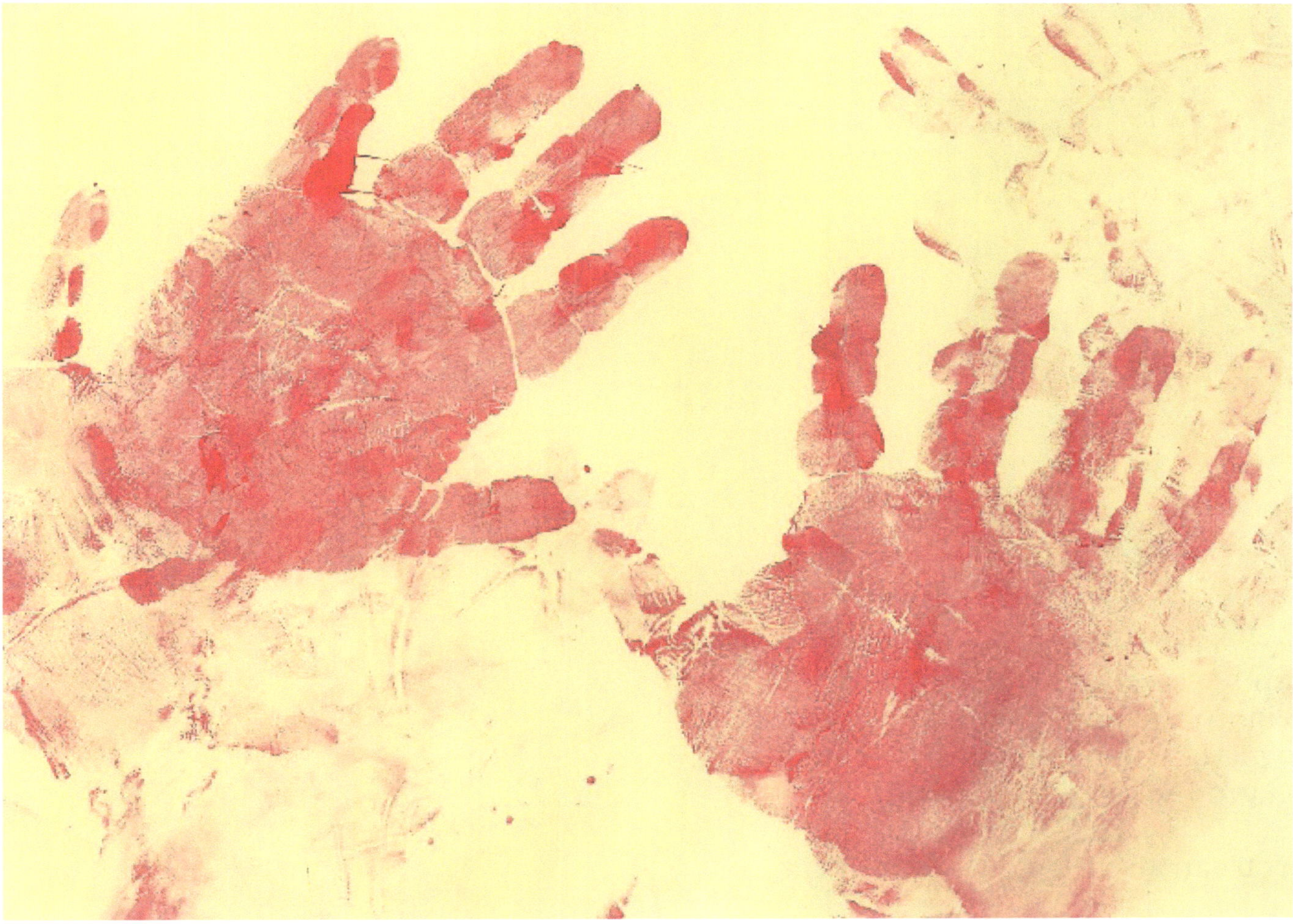

more interesting. Using several fabrics for the background will create a lovely change in texture because of the different fabrics. You should use the same method for choosing several red fabrics for the hands. It will make the quilt very interesting.

If you have a picture with smudges on the background like Exhibit F, I suggest getting rid of the smudges and make the pattern with the hands only. Here's how to do it:

3. Go into "Adjust Colors" and make the contrast greater. It will get rid of some of the smudges and will also make the hands more clear.

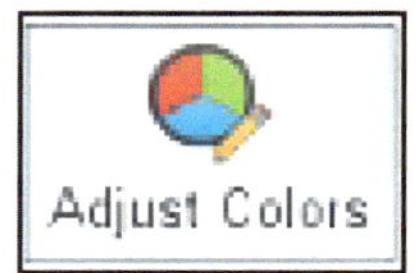

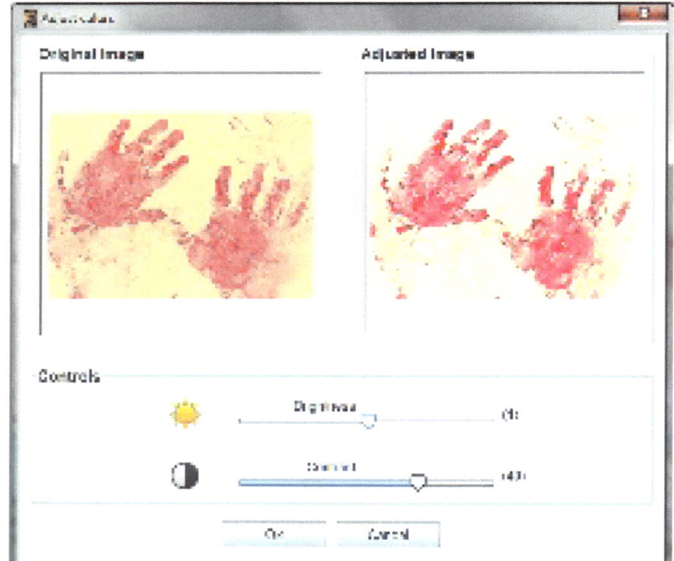

In this screen you will adjust the "Brightness" and "Contrast" to make the picture stand out clearly from the background.

4. You can also crop out some of the

Original Photograph

Restore Original

* Hold down left mouse button and drag cursor to crop the original photograph.

unwanted edges by dragging the cursor across the "Original Photograph" while holding down the left mouse button. You will be able to see your selected area highlighted by a red outline.

If you want to change the cropped area, you

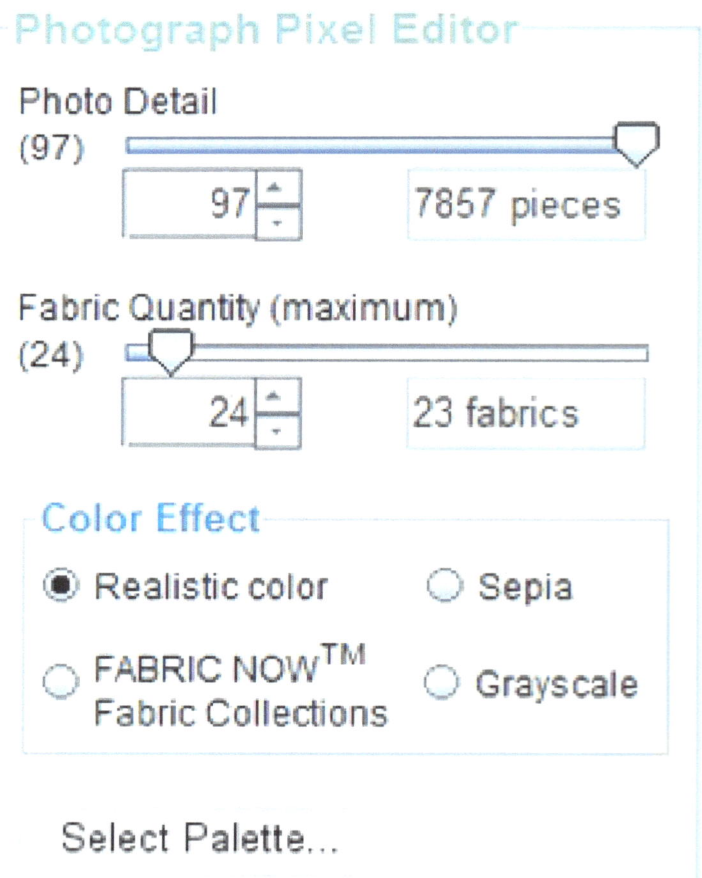

can restore the original picture by clicking the "Restore" button below the image.

5. The next thing you'll need to do is select your options in the "Photograph Pixel Editor."

Set the photo detail to a high number and also the fabric quantity above 24. Even though we only have two colors, we are setting the fabric quantity to a high number because we want the picture to be very clear. We want to see the hand edges and make a pattern that is easy to use. We also choose "Realistic Color" for the color effect.

You can take the "Photo Detail" up as high as the software will allow. The picture will be perfect and that's what we want for this technique.

If the edges of your picture look a bit unclear at this stage, don't worry because I will show you how to make them perfectly clear in chapter 6.

Push the "Process Image" button to see what the pattern will look like.

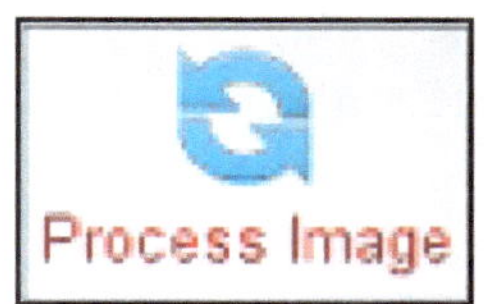

6. The next thing we're going to do is press "Print."

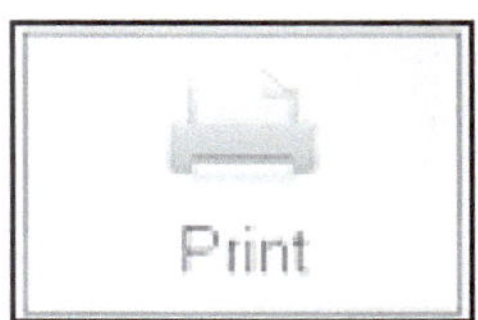

In the "Page Setup" window, you can change the "Size of Unit" and that will

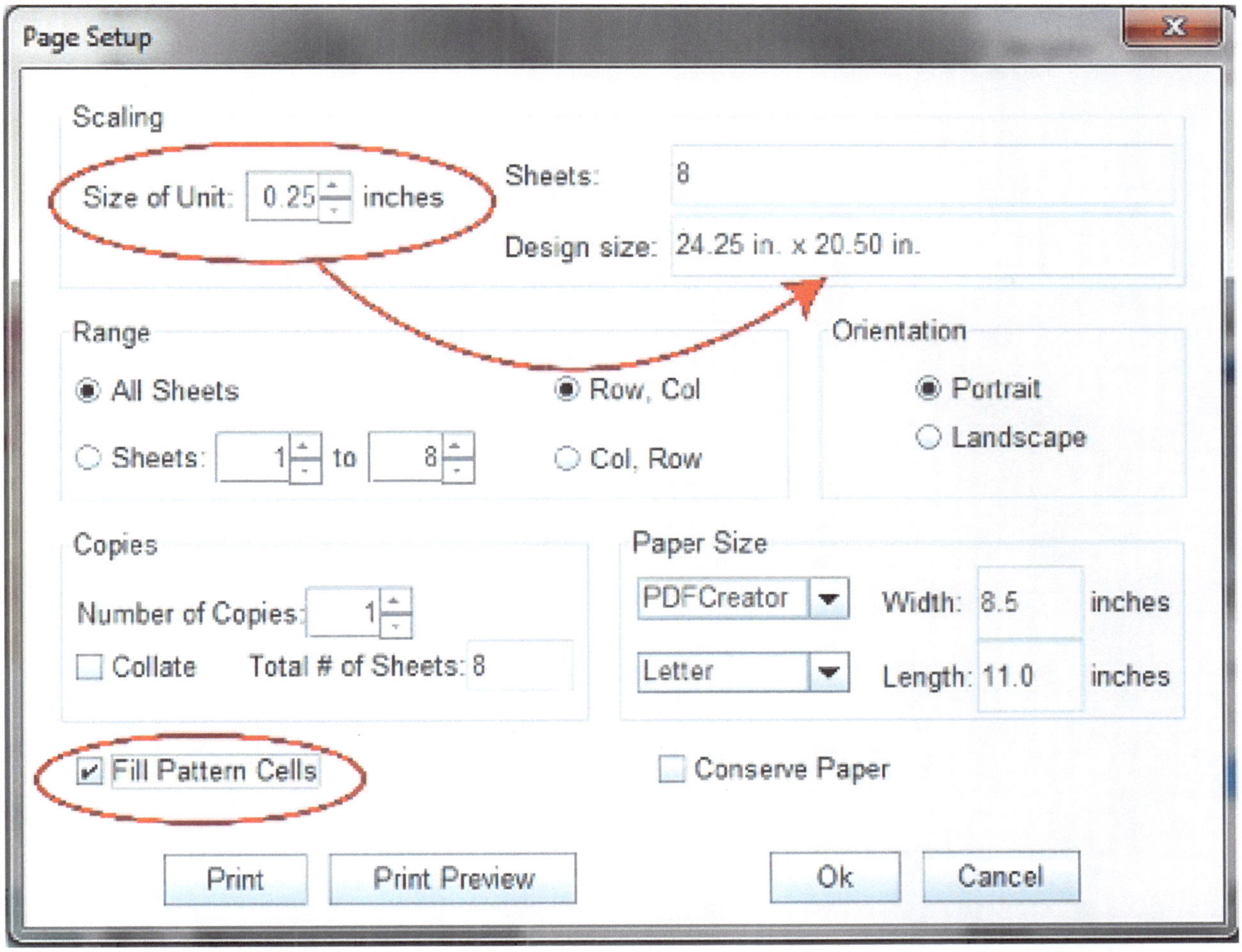

Page Setup
Scaling
Size of Unit: 0.25 inches
Sheets: 8
Design size: 24.25 in. x 20.50 in.
Range
All Sheets
Sheets: 1 to 8
Row, Col
Col, Row
Orientation
Portrait
Landscape
Copies
Number of Copies: 1
Collate
Total # of Sheets: 8
Paper Size
PDFCreator
Letter
Width: 8.5 inches
Length: 11.0 inches
Fill Pattern Cells
Conserve Paper
Print
Print Preview
Ok
Cancel

determine the size of each square. The reason why you change the square size is because it allows you to control the total size of the finished quilt/pattern. Play with the "Size of Unit " until you have the size you want.

When you change the unit size, you will automatically change the "Design Size". Note: After you change the "Size of Unit" , click inside the "Design Size" box to calculate the finished quilt/pattern size.

When you look on the lower left side of the page setup window, you will see an option to "Fill Pattern Cells" and that's what makes the correct style of pattern for this technique. Using this option will create a full color pattern that will allow you to see the picture perfectly.

The next step is to print the pattern and tape the pages together. See chapter 3 for details on how to tape the pattern pages together.

After you assemble all of the pages, get a pen or pencil to finish preparing your pattern. You'll outline the colored image

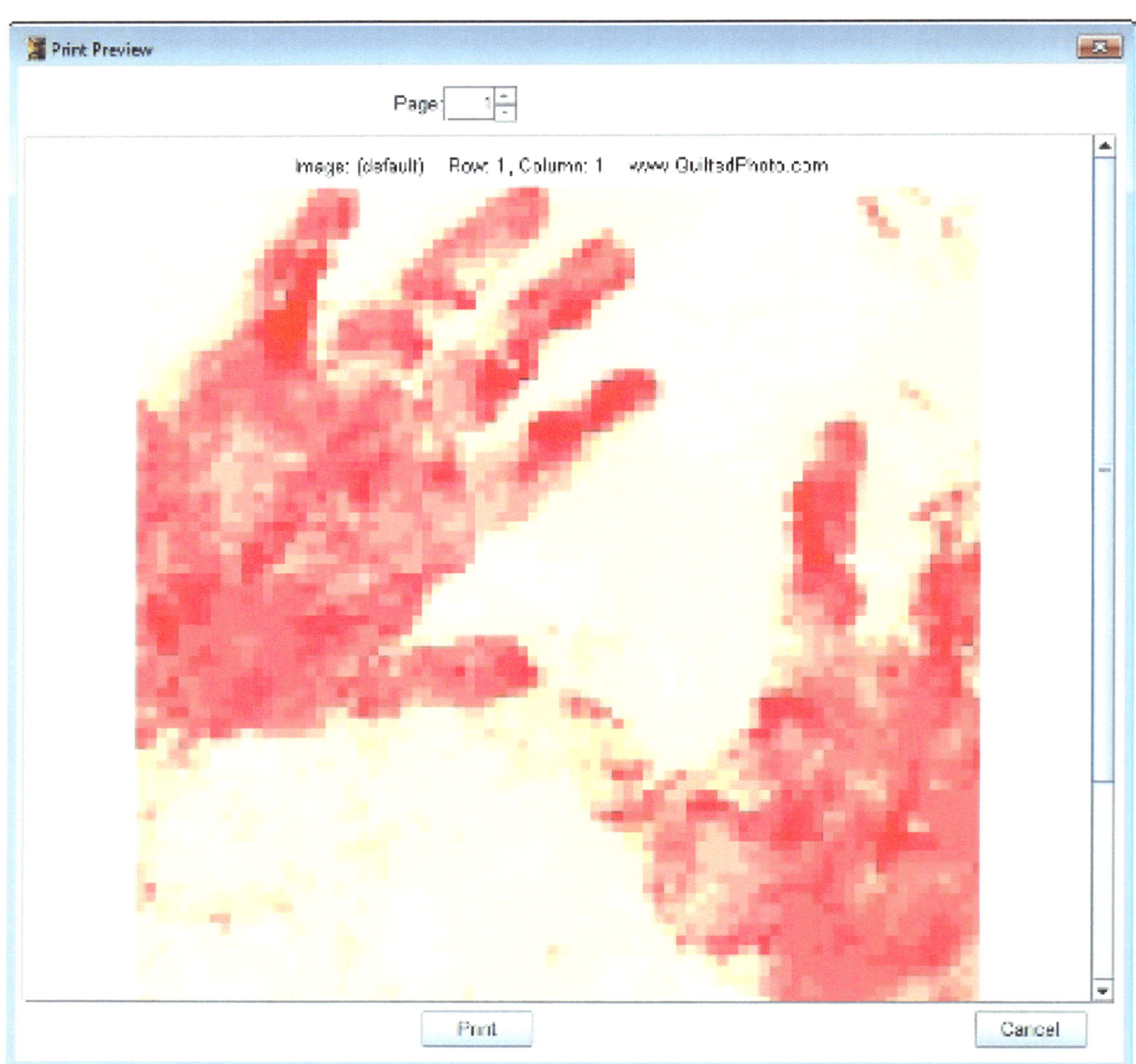

(on the paper pattern) ignoring any imperfections and smudges. That's going to give you all the detail you need. You can see every detail in the fingers. I would draw every detail, keeping the creases and all because it will make this image much better.

In other chapters, I will explain how to make patterns for several different possible types of drawings/paintings. I will do this because I want you to be able to understand and make all different types of drawings. These painted hands are just one particular type.

Now I want to summarize the important ideas so you'll know exactly how to proceed with the next step.

Idea #1 - Choose your artist. It can be your grandchild, it can be your child, it can be you, it can be anybody. Choose your artist.

Idea #2 - Get your artist to draw you a picture. Get yourself to draw yourself a picture. It can be a house, it can be a car, it can be anything. Draw whatever you like, as long as you make it simple with just a few colors.

Idea #3 - Make sure that you have only a few colors because we want simplicity. Simplicity doesn't mean it's going to be boring. Simplicity just means you have room to do amazing stitching and that is what makes your quilt really amazing.

Idea #4 - Follow the contours of the drawing or painting for the stitching!

Lastly, on the next few pages I have selected some drawings/paintings that are appropriate to make with this technique. I hope you will be inspired. These examples should give you ideas on the types of drawings that will make amazing stitched art!

Idea #5 - When you look at the pictures on the following pages, imagine them as big wall art or as giant art blankets!

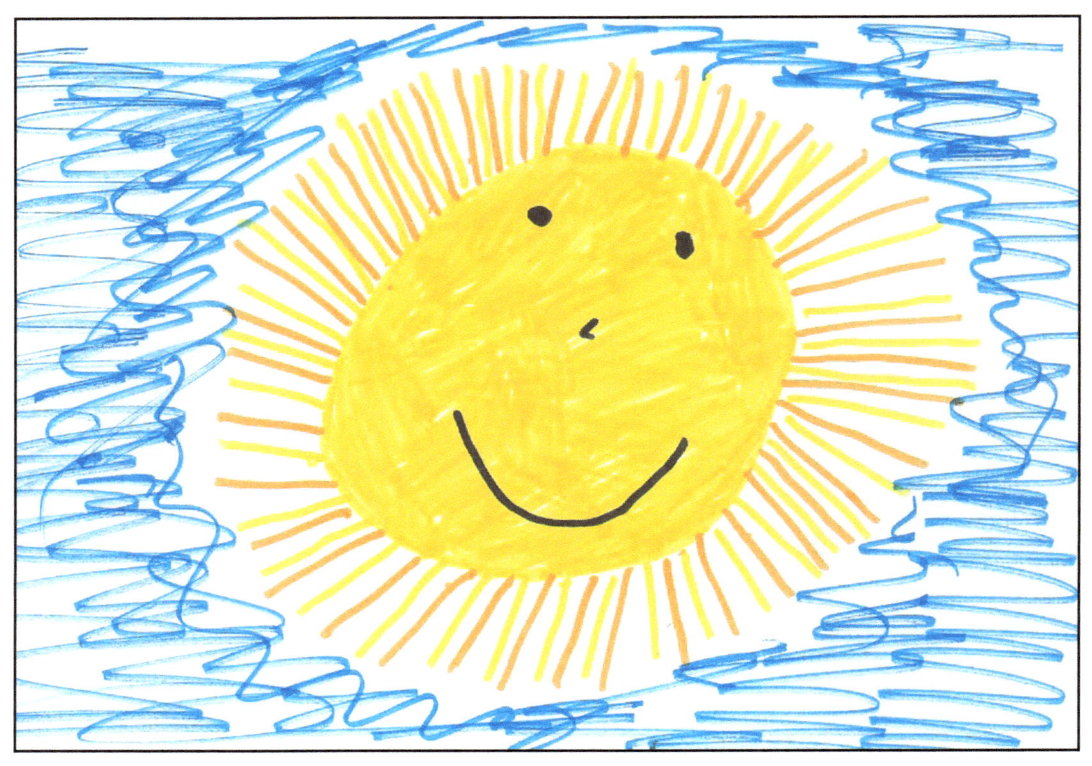

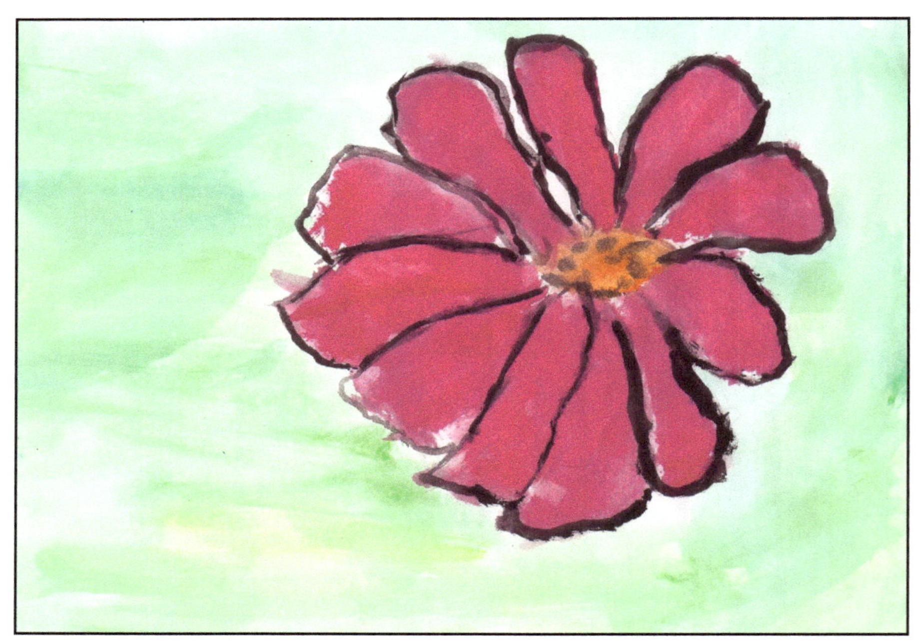

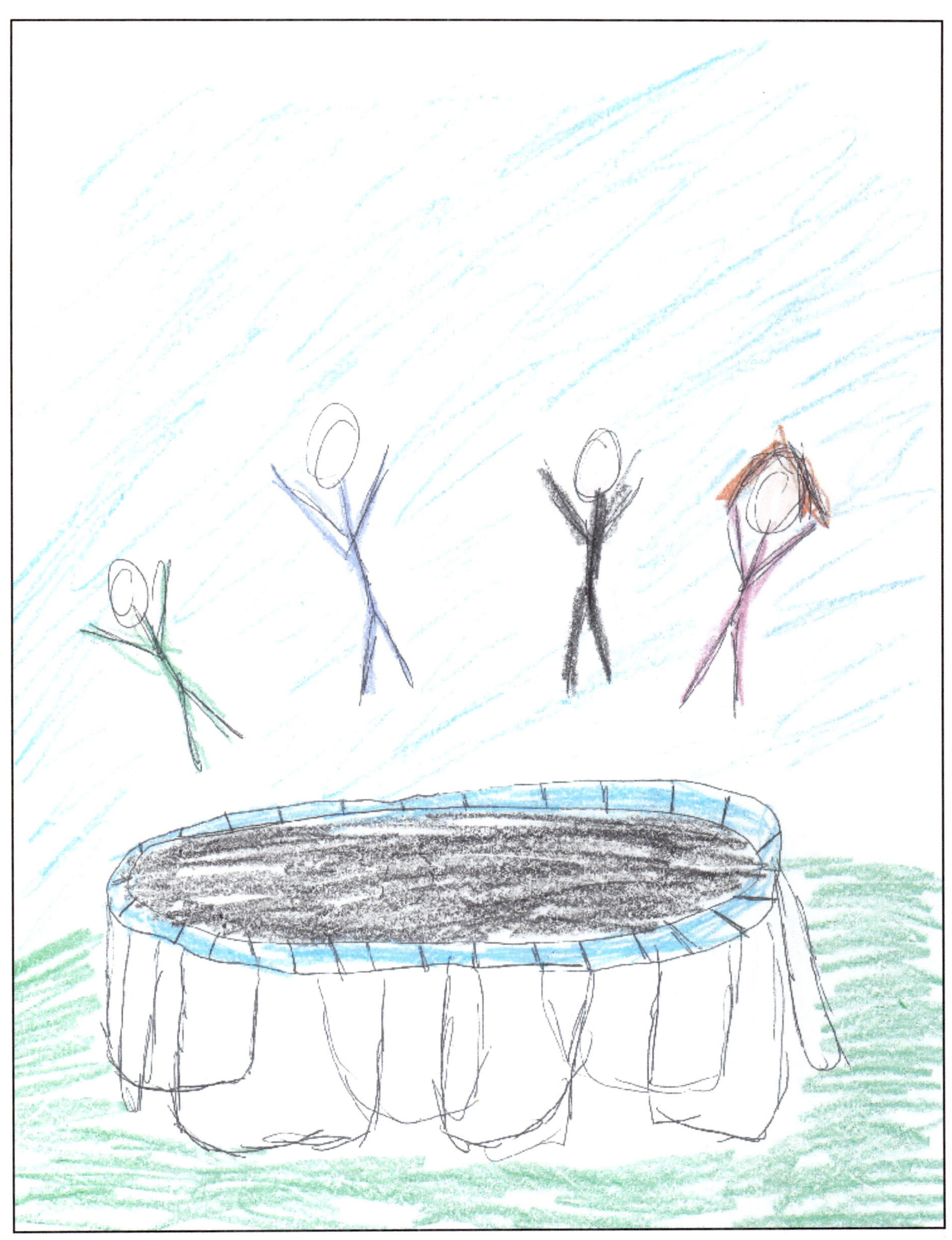

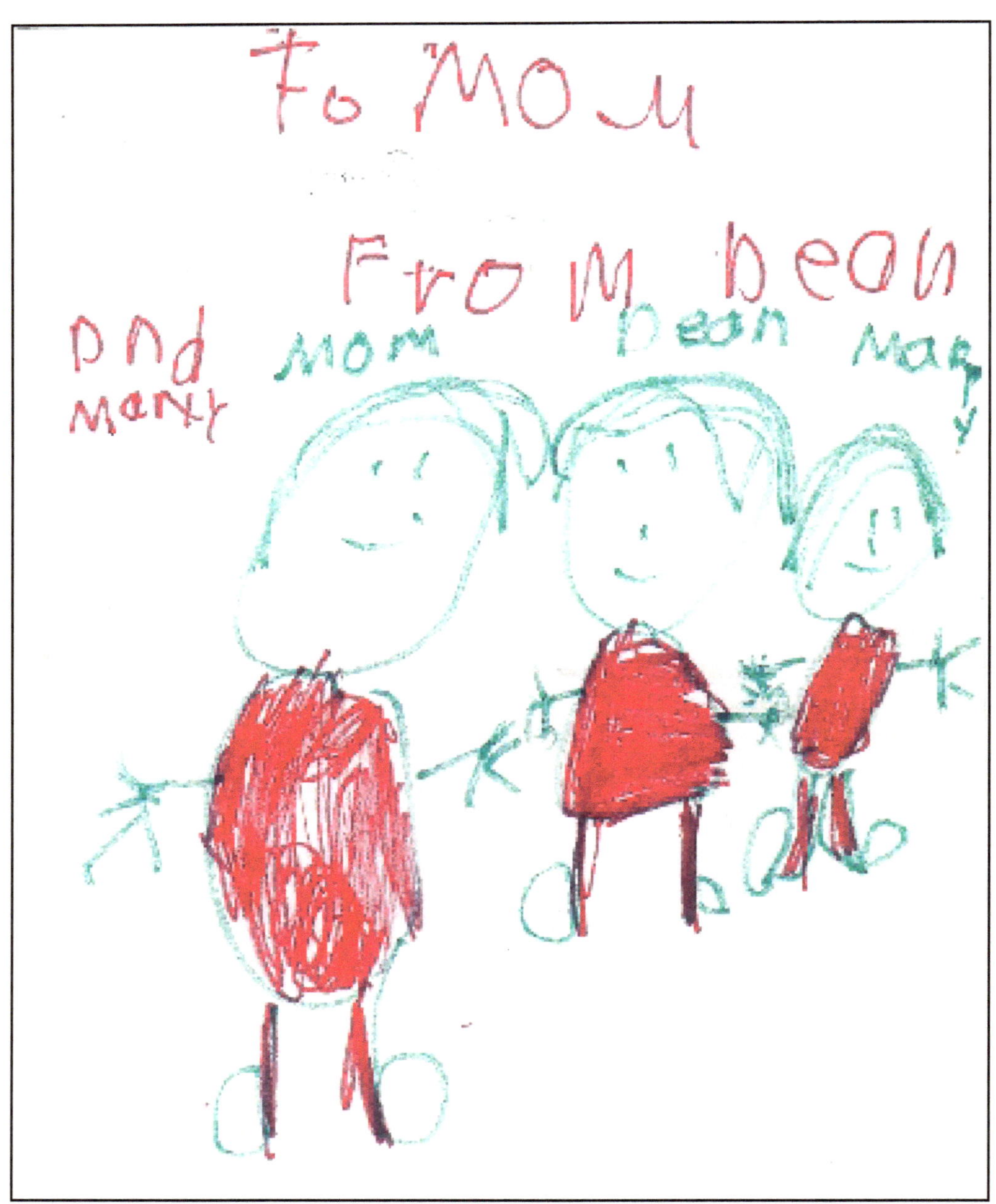
To MOM
From dean
and Mary
mom
dean
Mary

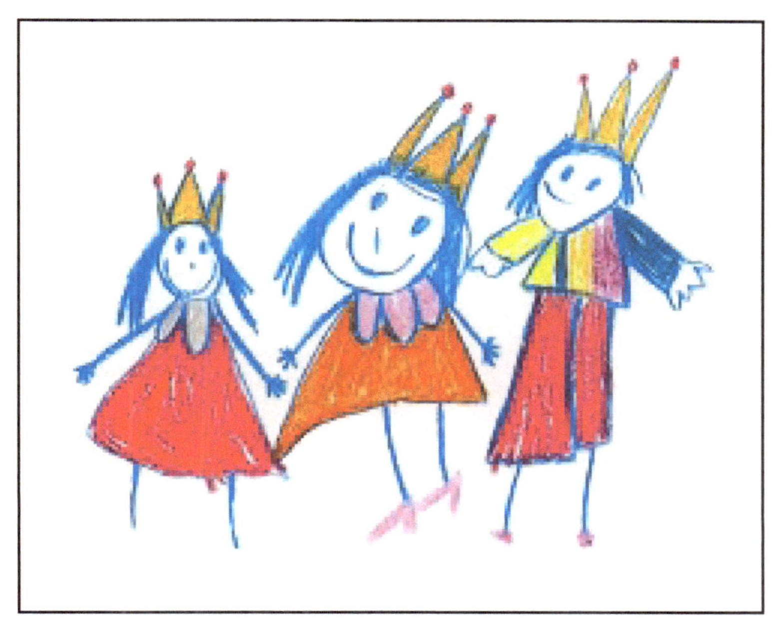

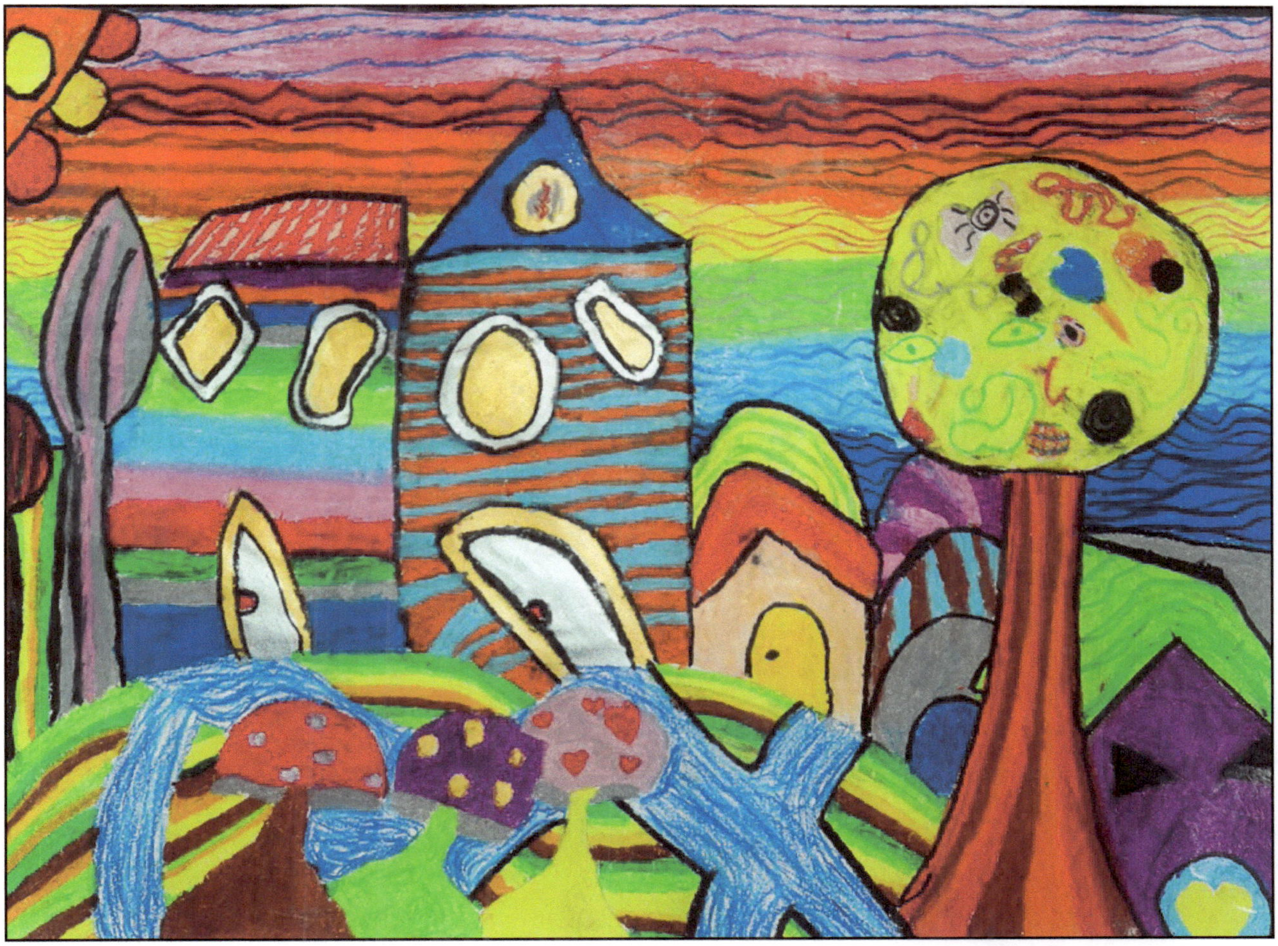

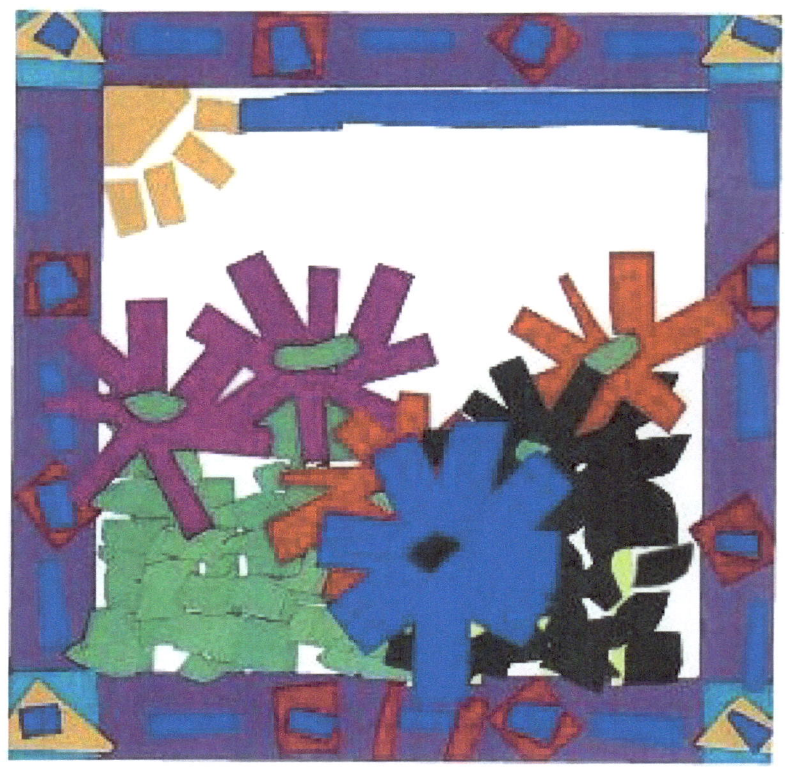

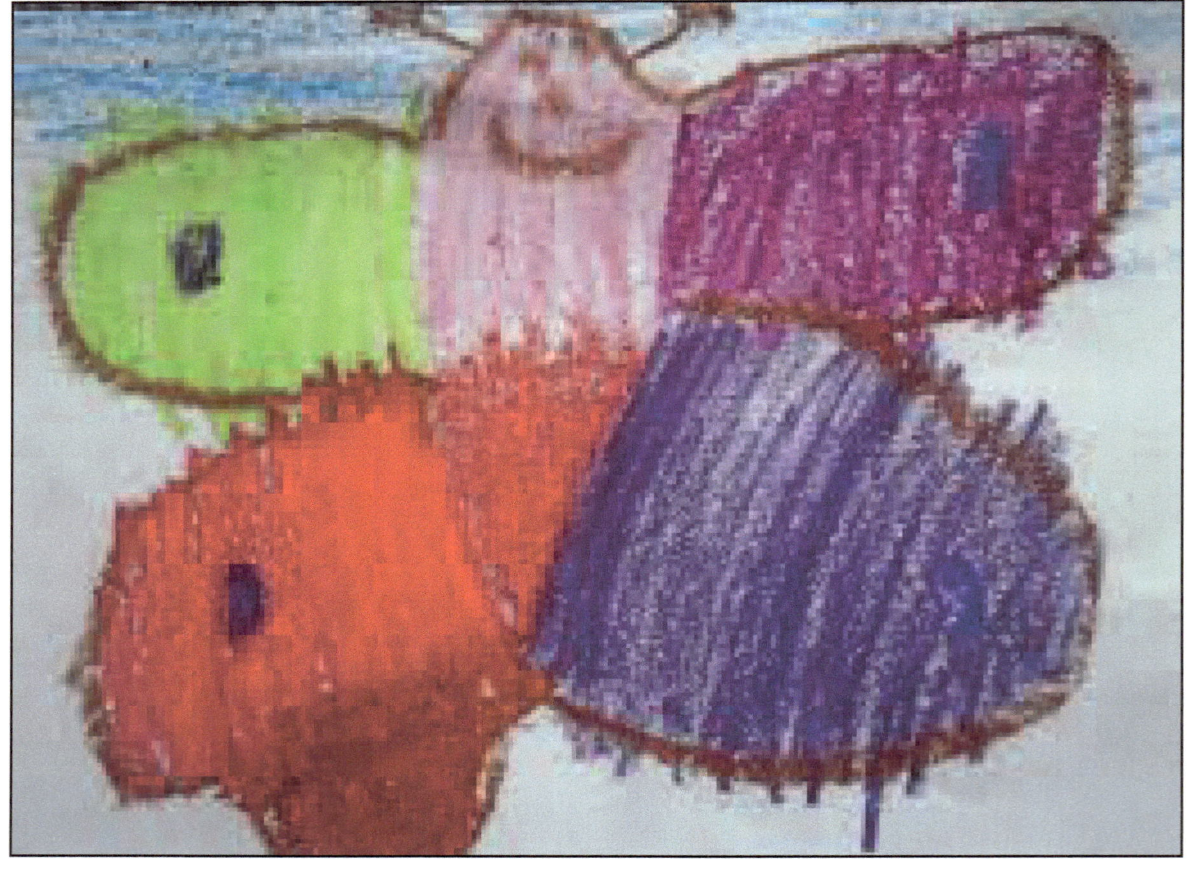

Chapter 2

Important Concepts

In this chapter, I want to show you two very important concepts that you must give your attention to for this technique to work.

Concept #1 is FOCUS and concept #2 is LAYERS. Understanding these two concepts will make this whole method very easy. You can use crayons or colored pencils to make something like [Exhibit G]. Remember to draw something simple.

Exhibit G is a happy drawing It's a simple drawing, but it can also be an amazing piece of art if you use Concept #1.

FOCUS
Exhibit G is a very nice picture. It looks like sunflowers, birds, sky, sunshine, and grass, but there are too many elements in the picture. It's much better if you create FOCUS by cropping out some of it and just keep a few of the elements. That's what I have done in Exhibit H. Removing some of the elements will make the picture much better for this technique. Cropping increases the picture FOCUS and makes the project simple.

Exhibit G

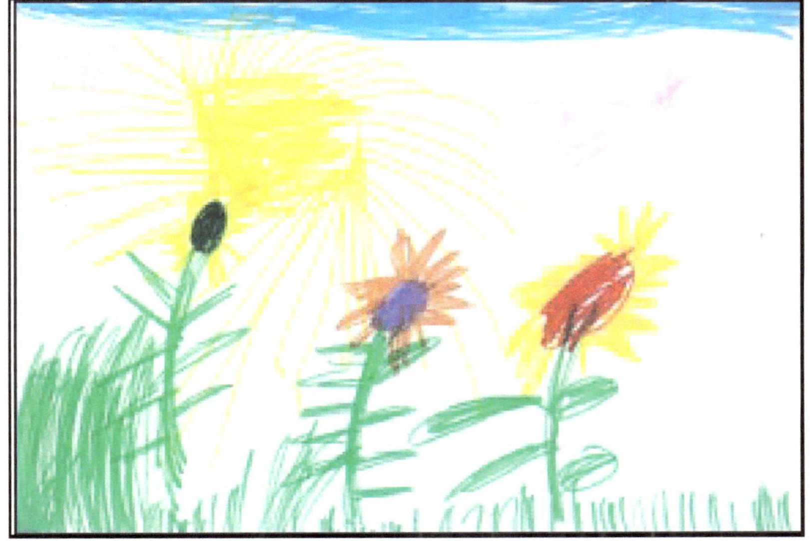

Exhibit I (on the next page) is a perfectly good picture as well, but it also has too many elements. It's better if you choose just a portion of the picture to create better FOCUS. Remember to choose simplicity over complicated.

Now I'm going to talk about concept #2, and this is where it gets exciting.

LAYERS
Take a close look at the picture to notice the elements and how they will be best represented. This tip requires a little bit of planning.

Exhibit H

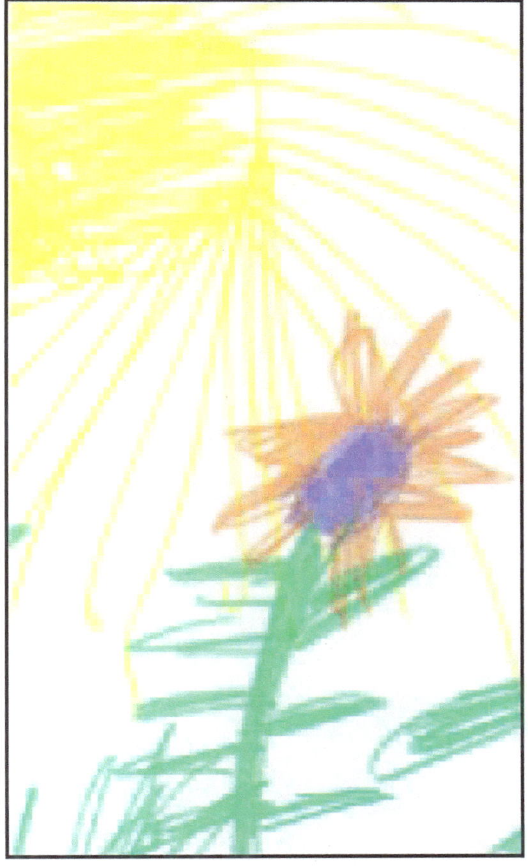

Example I

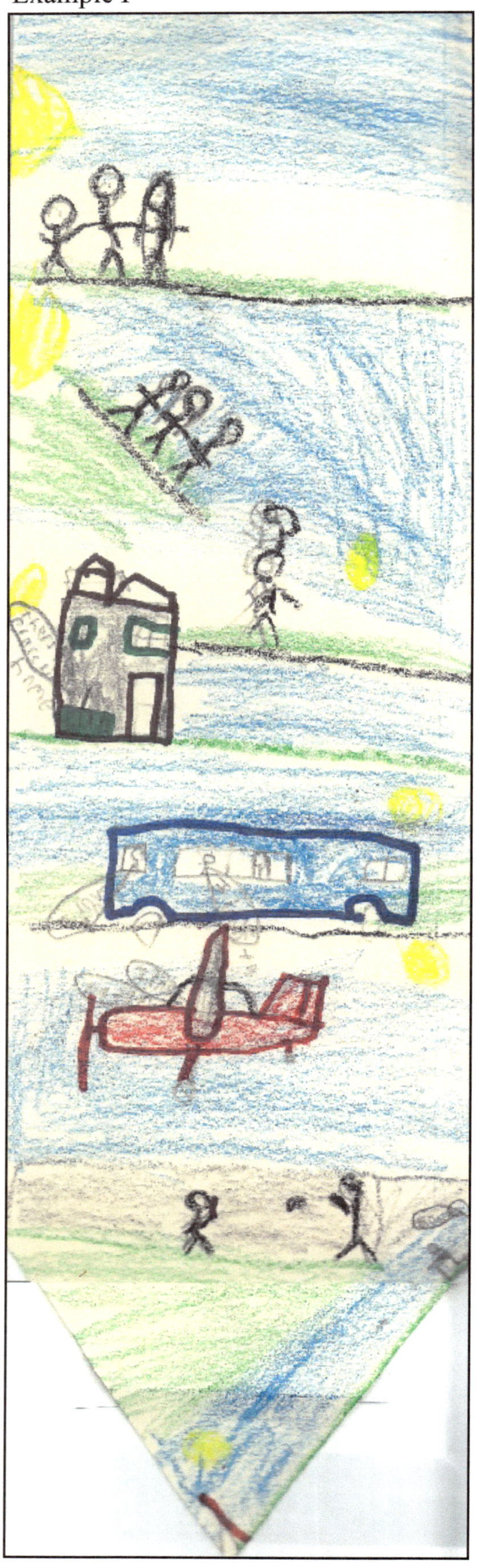

With layers in mind, take a look at Exhibit J below. As you can see, it has a beige background, it has lime green, blue and white feathers that are on top of the background, then the body of the bird on top of that.

The easiest way to achieve the look of this drawing is to create some parts of the picture as stitching on top instead of fabric pieces. In my opinion, the black around the edges of the body

Exhibit J

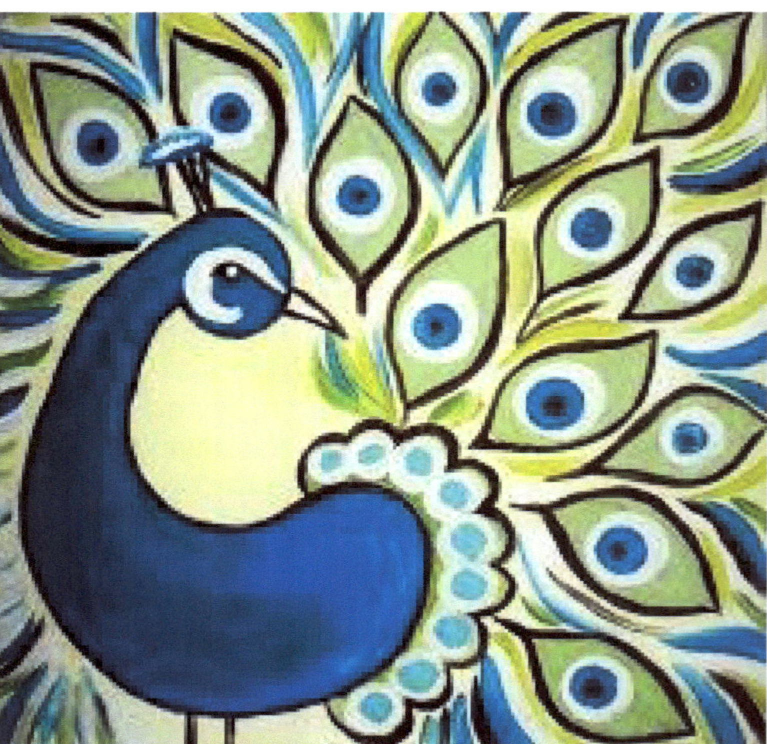

and flowers should be stitched in black. Even some of the blue strokes can also be stitched. I think that's the best way to do it.

All of these layers require a little bit of thought ahead of time. Planning is what will allow you to be successful without making too many mistakes.

Exhibit K is another fantastic image. This is a tree in silhouette. If I were going to try to cut out between all of these branches, that would be a nightmare, but with a little bit of planning, you can do all the thin parts of the branches in stitching and it will becomes very simple and a more interesting piece of art.

Exhibit K

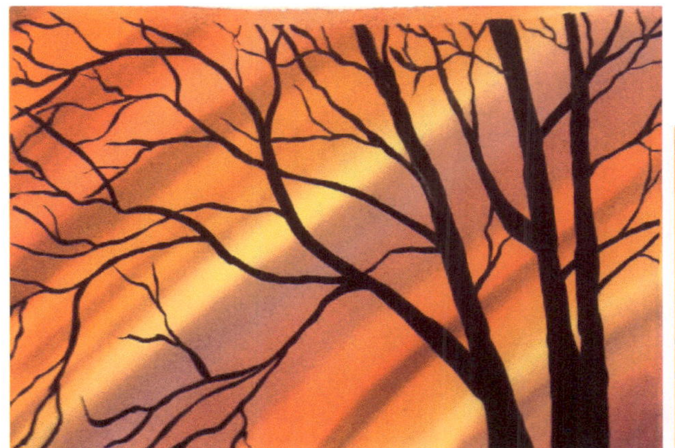

I would cut out the thick branches and the trunk of the tree in fabric, but I would do all of the little skinny branches in stitching.

The best tool for this process is "Quilting Film". It is inexpensive and you can get it on my website.

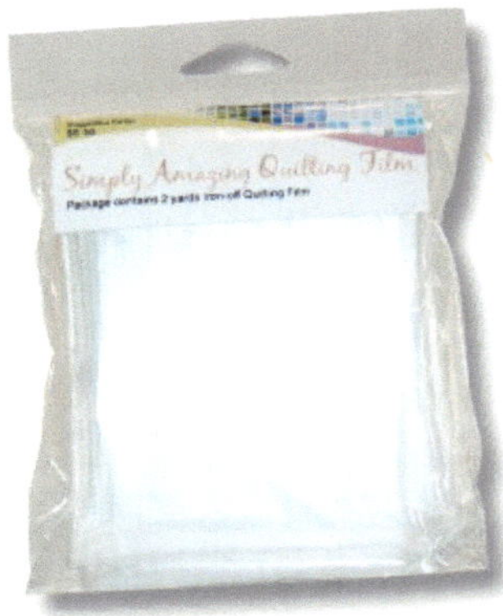

This is a quick overview of how to use it: First of all, It looks like a clear plastic, but it's not regular plastic. Put it right over the top of your pattern. Then you use a sharpie. to map out your stitching plan right on the quilting film. You can write on the clear film and clearly view your fabric underneath. If you make a mistake, you can wipe away the mistake with a damp napkin and start over. Once finished, you'll be able to see exactly where you're going to stitch. You will essentially make a stitching map for yourself. View details for using quilting film on page 52.

Exhibit L

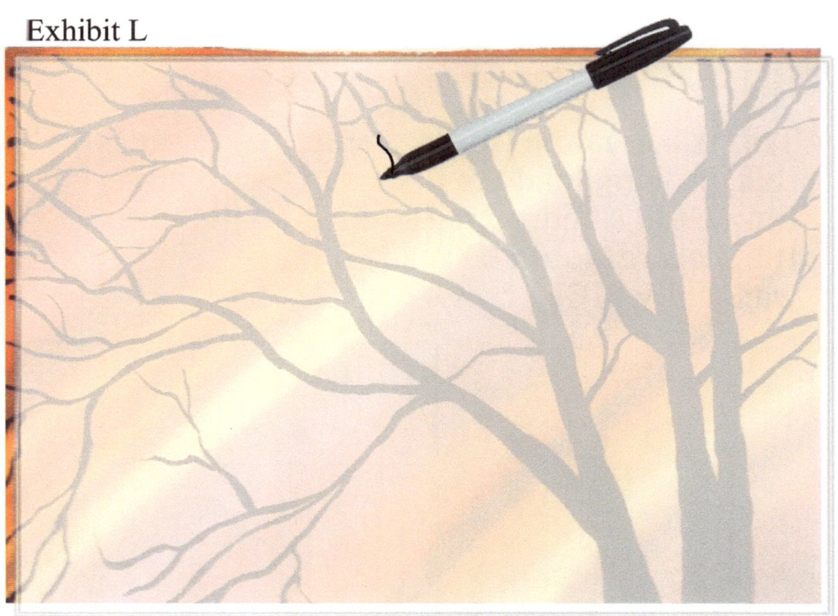

What's nice about this method is that if you're afraid of your fabric lifting up, it doesn't happen. The film holds all the pieces flat and firmly in place. The film/map also lets you know where to stitch, so you don't have to guess. On page 52, I will give more details on how to use the quilting film.

Lets look at another picture while we are still talking about layers. When you look closely at Exhibit M (on the next page) you will notice that it's made of triangles and little scallops. Those shapes would be cut as fabric pieces. The skinny arms, the hair, smiley faces and outlines would all be stitched with thread.

Exhibit M

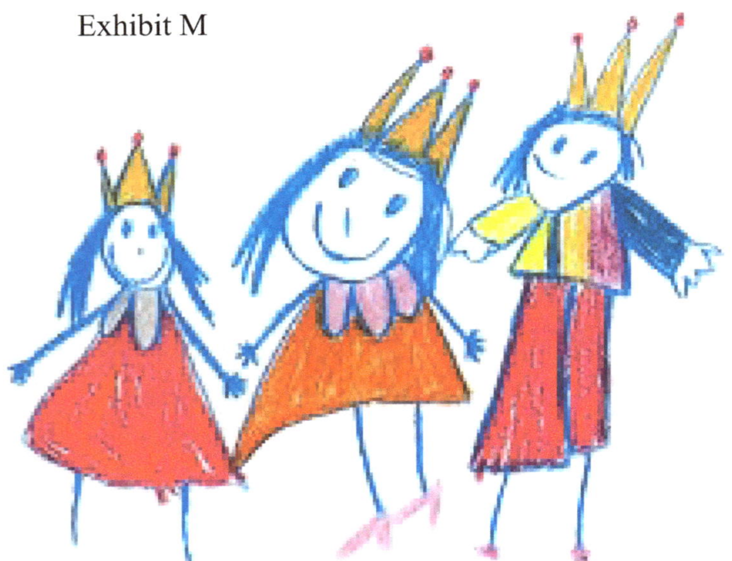

When you look at Exhibit N, it seems as though it would only require 3 fabrics, but you can make the picture more interesting by using several fabrics of each color. For example, I would choose many different pink fabrics of diverse textures and all of those textures together would make it very interesting. I would choose several fabrics for the green background and orange flower center the same way and of course, all of the outlines would be created with stitching.

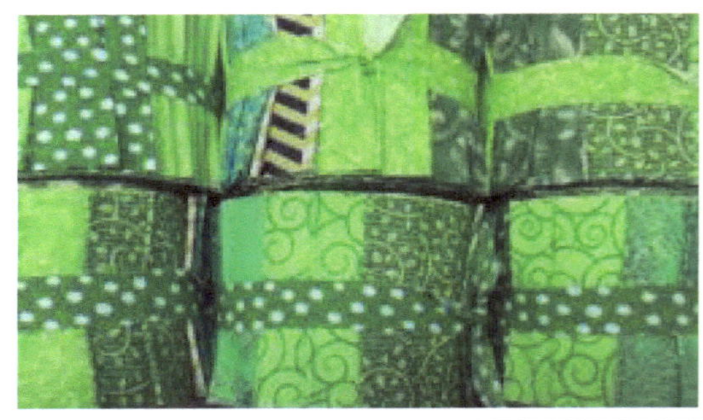

This is a great picture! I would like to see this drawing made really large, as a blanket for a child's bedroom. It's cute small, but the picture would be really amazing if it was really BIG!

Exhibit N

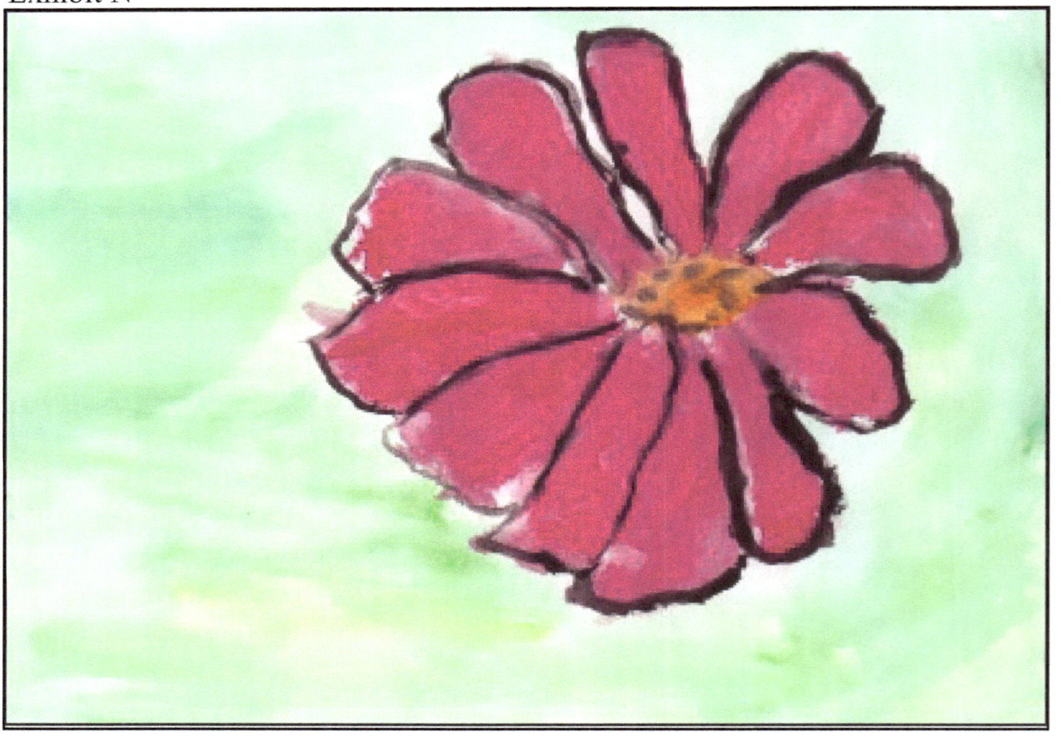

I'll show you exactly how to make a larger sized blanket in chapter 6. The reason I love this drawing is because of it's beautiful simplicity.

You can see some of the paint strokes in the drawing (Exhibit N). The directions of the strokes give clear instruction on the exact location and in exactly what direction to stitch.

We'll go into more detail in chapter 5 on exactly how to choose your fabric, but right now we're talking about selecting multiple fabrics for each color to make the quilt much more interesting than it would be with a single fabric per color.

Exhibit O

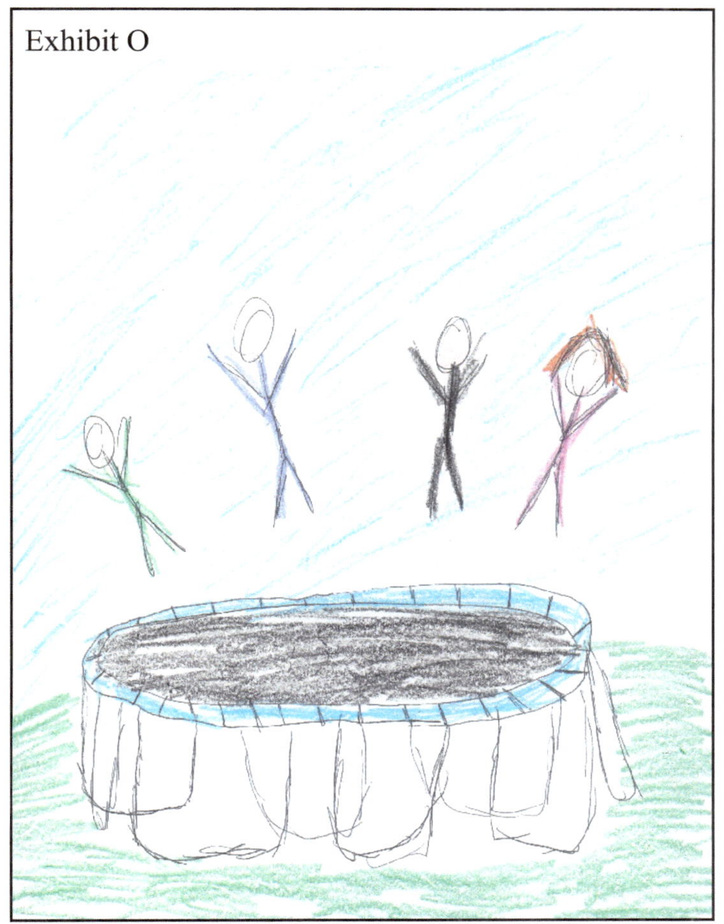

Now I have a couple of questions for you. Are you thinking about layers? Do you understand how to simplify a picture and identify the elements? What parts of this picture should be background and what do you think should be the stitching on Exhibit O?

Exhibit O would be very easy. This is the way I would do it. I would choose a light colored background and then I would stitch all of the scribbles as stitching. I would follow the direction of the crayon lines and I try to do as much of it as possible exactly like the drawing.

I would also do this whole area under the trampoline in a lighter color and all of the legs would be the stitching, including all of the detail around the edge of the trampoline. I would use a darker color fabric on the top of the trampoline. The little round face pieces would be some sort of beige color or peachy color or brown color. For all of the rest of the details, I would use stitching.

The picture has the detailed areas in several different colors - green, purple or blue, black and pink. One of the little people has red hair and all of the bodies and trampoline legs have different colors. Well, I would change the thread color for each item to keep the picture exactly as the original drawing.

I wish I knew the story to this one because it makes it much more fun when you know the story that goes with picture. I would ask the artist what they were thinking about and was that a real day? Were they really jumping on trampolines? Who were those people? That's one of the things I really like about children's drawings. They always have a fun story and it's a great way to remember the stories for later.

I want to show you another tree picture (Exhibit P on the next page).

This tree doesn't have to be exactly the colors that the original painting was. You can choose whatever colors you want on a painting like this.

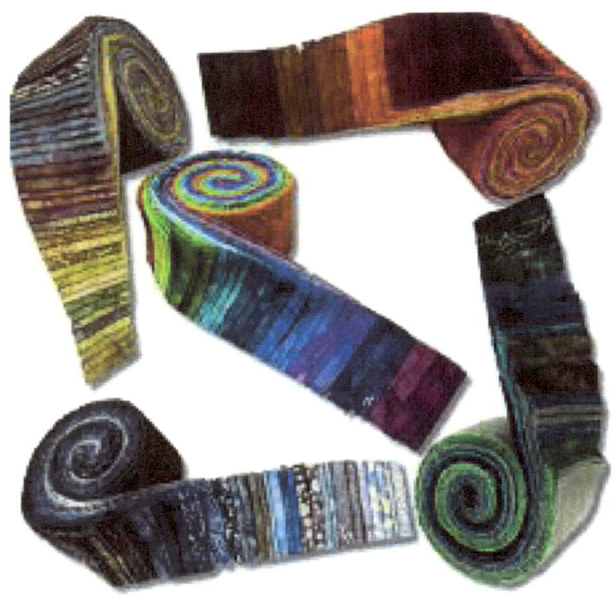

The little jellyrolls (above) would be perfect for a quilt like Exhibit P. One jellyroll would supply you with a wide assortment of beautiful related fabrics. You can choose the perfect fabrics that you think are beautiful.

What's nice about most jellyrolls is that the colors in the fabrics are designed to coordinate nicely together. They're beautiful and that is what I would choose for a picture like Exhibit P.

My strategy for this quilt would be to cut the large part of the trunk in an appropriate fabric, stopping where it gets thin. Then to complete the end of the branch, I would finish the branch with stitching. All of the different colored sections would be cut from various fabrics. This picture would be amazing as a quilt.

I really like Exhibit Q. I like it because a young child made it and I know it has meaning to him.

I would choose lots of different blues for this amazing sky and a few bright red fabrics for the barn. Of course, I would choose a contrasting thread to make the details like the edge of the buildings and windows.

One thing I do want to mention about this particular picture is, I would never choose plain white for the background

Exhibit P

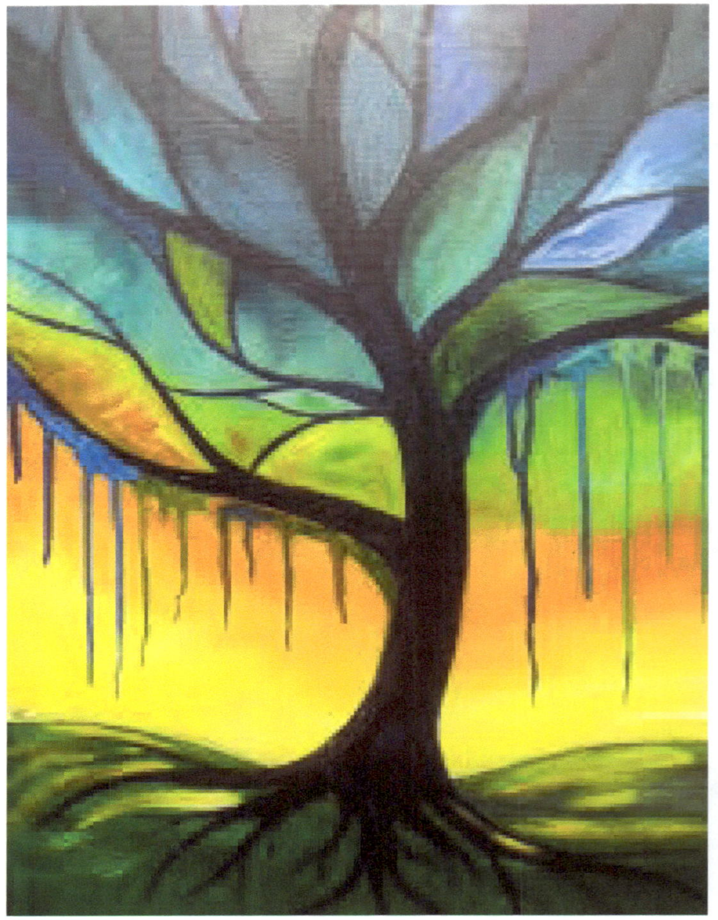

Exhibit Q

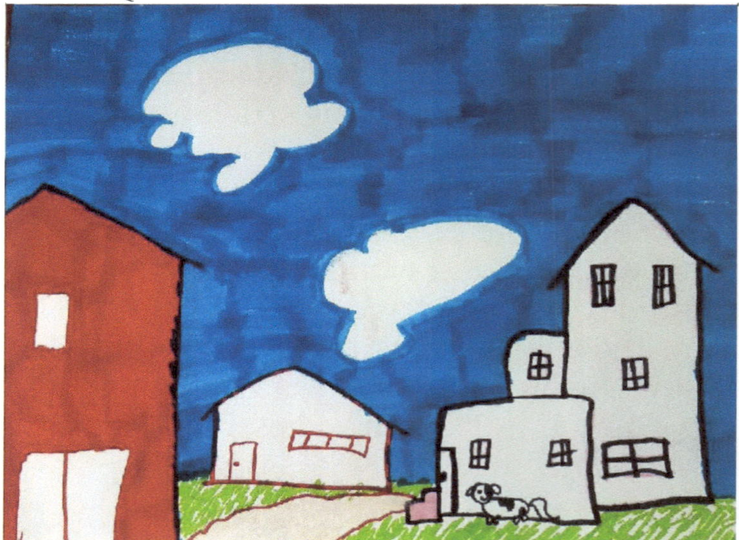

fabric because the white background is an opportunity to apply several beautiful light colored fabrics. I would choose an assortment of very light fabrics.

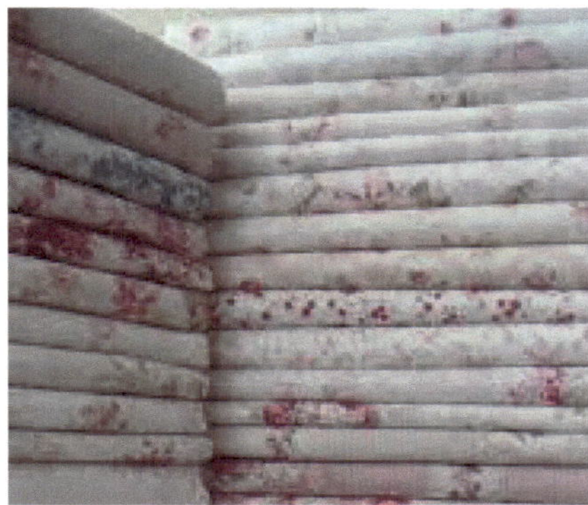

When I first saw Exhibit R, I was a little stumped. This drawing was made by a student and at first glance I thought it was complicated. But when I looked at it a little closer, I noticed that it's just the background that seems complicated.

Exhibit R

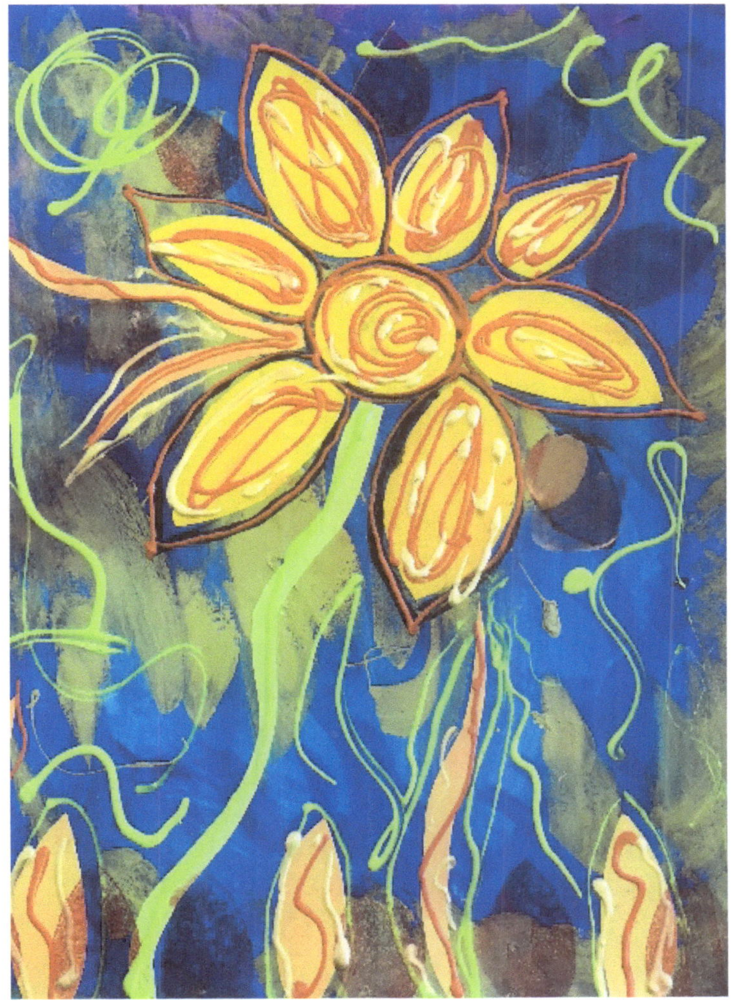

To mimic the background, I would choose fabrics that already kind of look like the background. Here are a few fabric ideas that would work for this purpose.

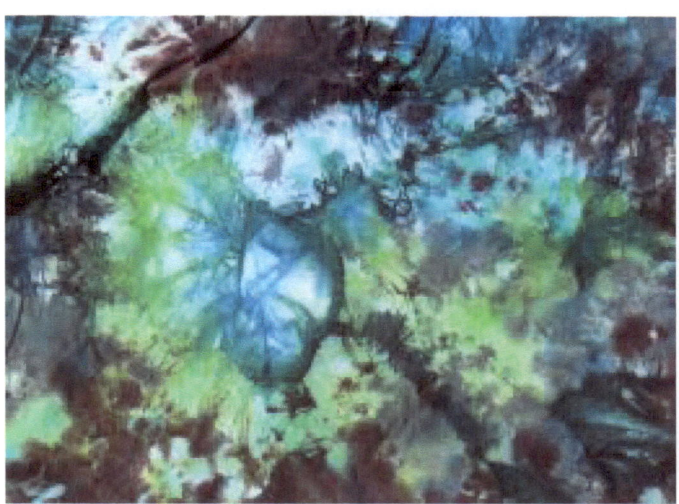

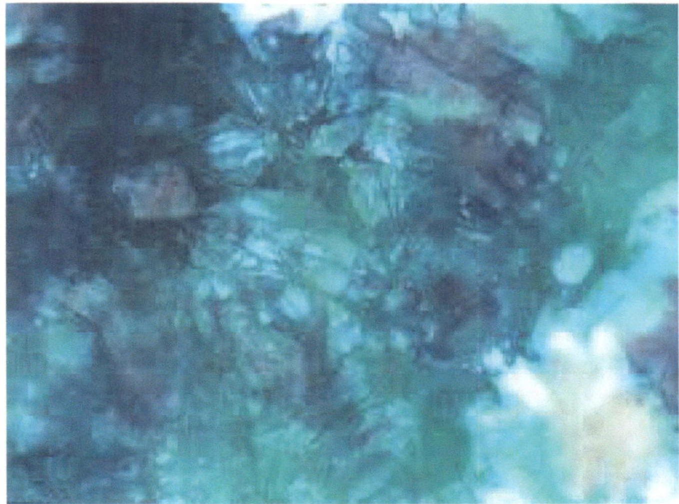

Once you identify the background, the rest of the picture is very simple. You have the yellow petals, of the flower and also the stem and the other pedal-like shapes at the bottom. I would use fabric for those and put them on top of the background. All the rest of these squiggly lines are just stitching. Remember to change the thread to match the colors of the original drawing. This picture is really very simple.

Exhibit S

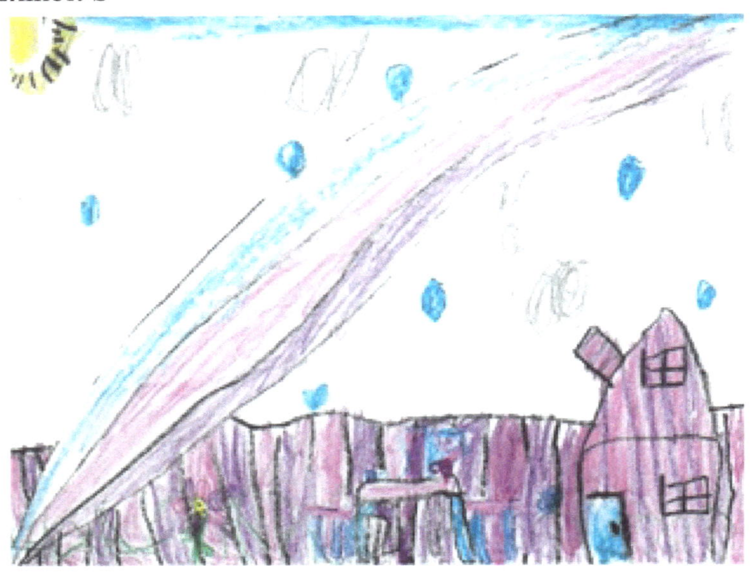

Exhibit S is another drawing from a young artist. When I see a drawing like this, that is mostly one color, (this picture has a lot of purple and a little aqua) I would start by referncing the color wheel. You will see that all of the purples and the aquas are on one side of the color wheel and directly across from them are the yellows and oranges.

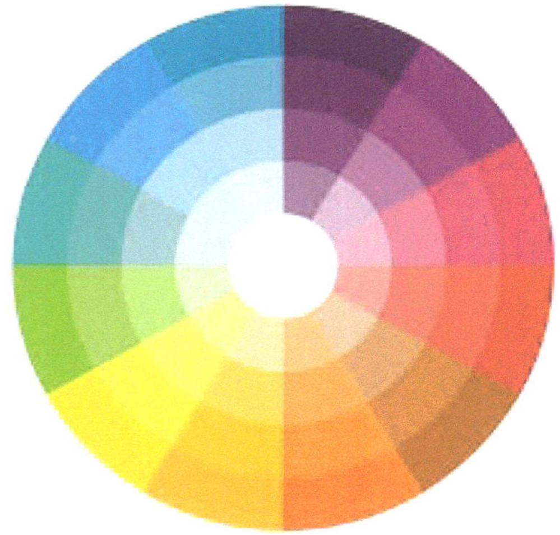

As a general rule, when colors are directly opposite from one another, both colors are highlighted. So, with that rule in mind, I would use a pale yellow or pale orange as the background color because the yellow/ orange will make the purple look more beautiful. That would make the purple look even more purple and the aqua look even more aqua.

You should also notice that the house seems to be blending into the fence. To make a bit more contrast, I would make the fence in a darker purple and in contrast, I would use a lighter lavender for the house and all the other items in front of the fence as well. Creating contrast will cause all of the elements to be more clear. Of course the smoke from the chimney would be created with stitching. With these color choices, this picture would be lovely.

Exhibit T

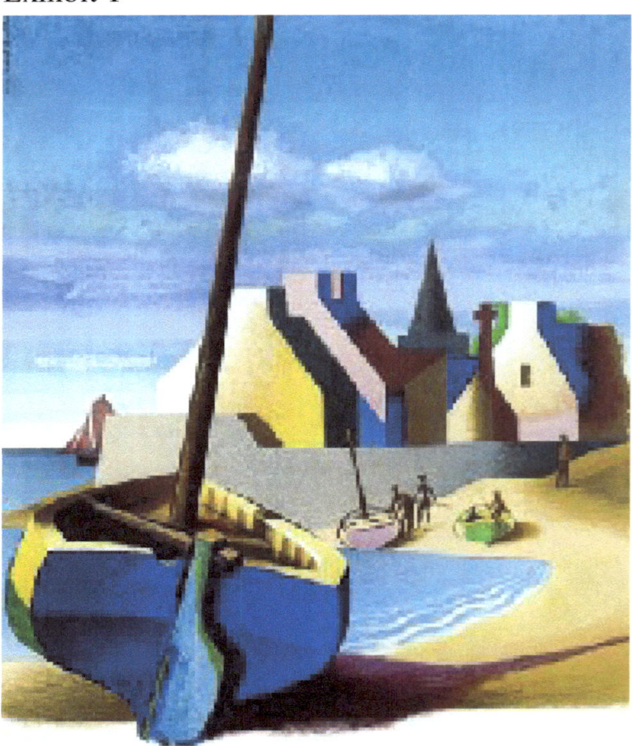

Lastly, I'm going to talk about Exhibit T. This picture is a little bit more sophisticated. First of all, the small details like the little people can be created with stitching. As for the buildings and everything else, you would get fabric with the gradation of color already built-in.

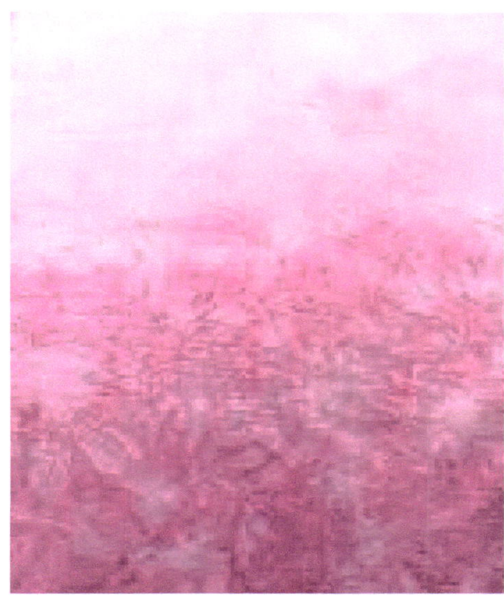

Notice the color of the buildings. The building in the center of the painting is a gradation from gold that gradually fades to white. You can choose fabrics that gradually change from one color to another as shown in the example fabrics above. You would cut them so that the gradation or change of color matches the gradations in the original picture. I want to mention the foamy waves on the shore of the water. I would create it with stitching. I would also create the boat shadows with stitching because the thread will make the shadows look transparent. For this type of picture, the key is to find fabrics that already have the gradations built into them.

I've used this picture to make a video software demo in my online class. The demonstration will make it clear how to make the patterns for this technique and what you should be looking for. You can see the video demo for free because you purchased this book. Go to page 88 for instruction on how to get your free online video course and trial software.

How To Make Patterns

You can use Quilted Photo Xpress 5.0 or Quilted Photo Xpress 5.0 software for this style of quilting. I will be using Quilted Photo Deluxe 2.0 for this demonstration. If you do not have either of these programs, you can download Quilted Photo Xpress 5.0 software free for 7-days! Go to page 88 to learn how to get it.

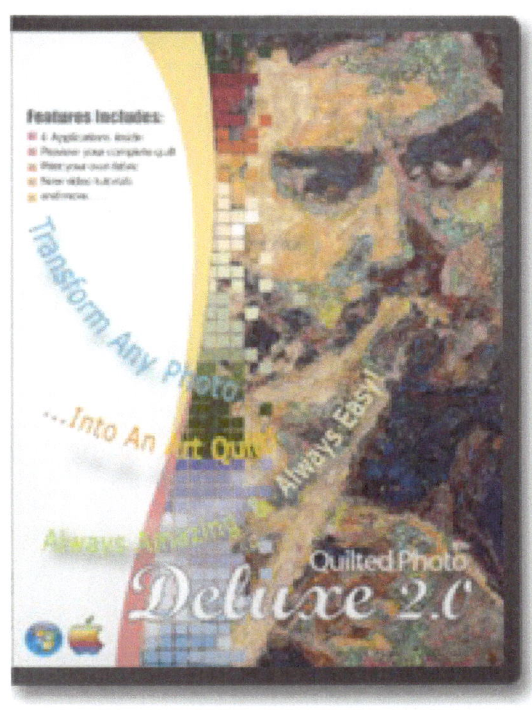

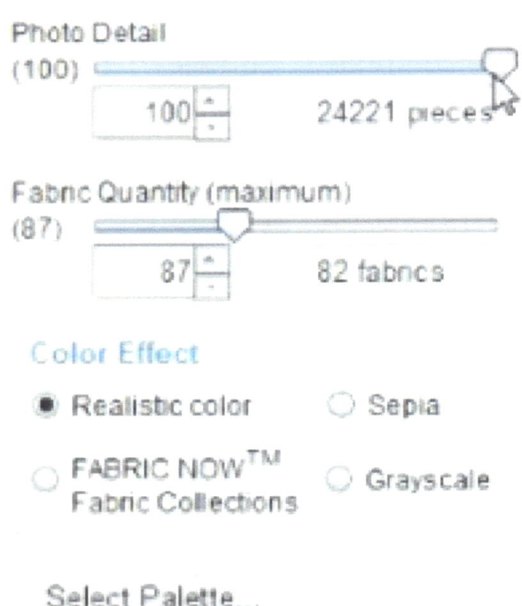

When you open the software on your computer, the first thing you will see is the "Pixel Editor". I adjusted the settings to levels that I would never use for any of my other techniques. I put the photo detail all the way up to 100 and I put fabric quantity up to 82. I've done that because for this technique, we're not going to cut individual pieces, nor 82 fabrics! What we are looking for is a clear "Processed Photograph". When you set both the "Photo Detail" and the "Fabric Quantity" to higher numbers, the result is a very clear "Processed Photograph".

When the "Processed Photograph" is clear on the screen, the clear pattern will make it possible to replicate the painting exactly.

Please note that I've also set the "Color Effect" to realistic color.

Color Effect

Realistic color　Sepia

FABRIC NOW™ Fabric Collections　Grayscale

If you are using "Quilted Photo Deluxe", do not click the contour tab for this technique. It's not designed to work for this method. You can select any of the pixel shapes you want, but square or 45 degree angle is perfect for this technique.

Original Photograph

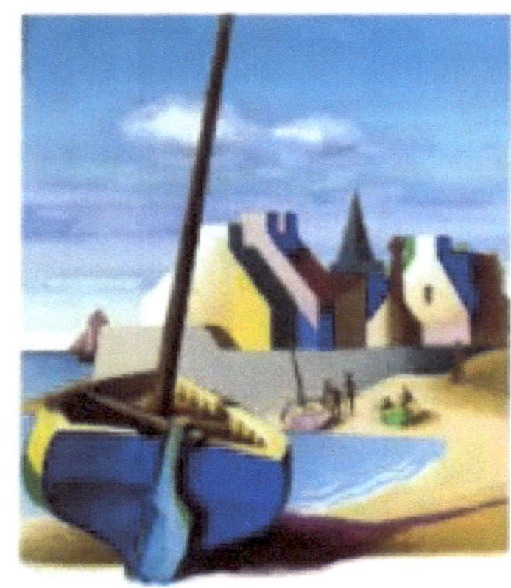

Processed Photograph

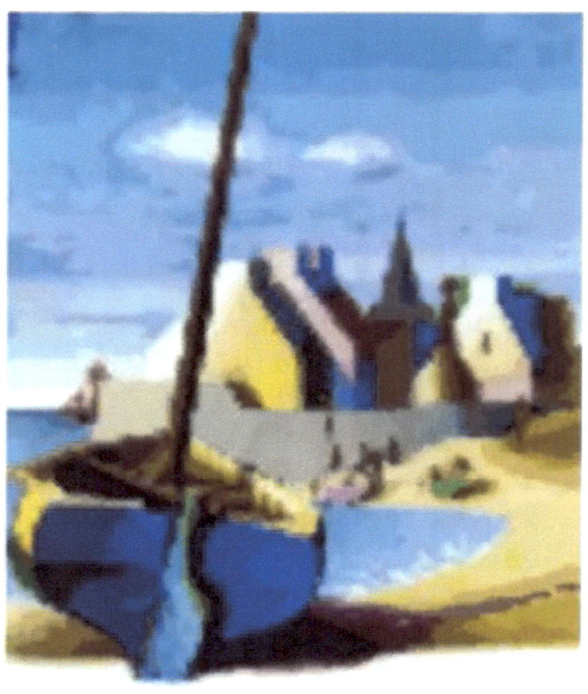

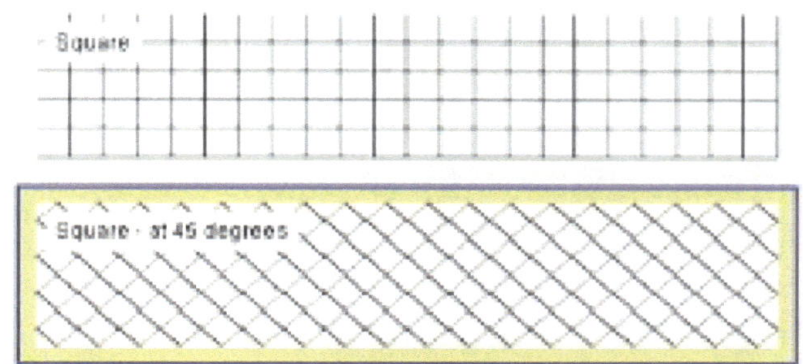

You don't need to use any other options on any of these other tabs.

Now is the time to click "Process Image".

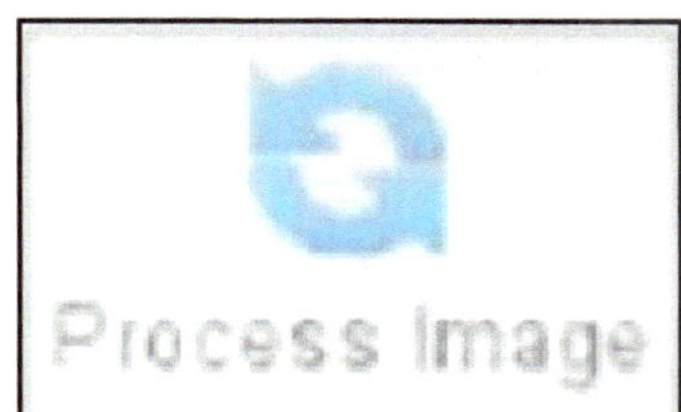

Then click the "Print" button.

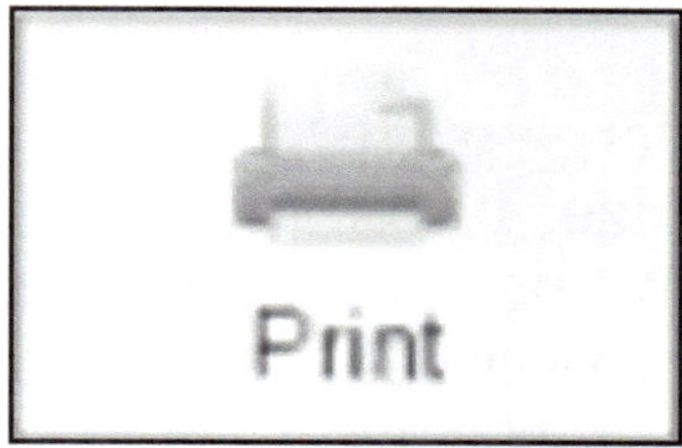

After you click the "Print" button, the "Page Setup" window will open.

The first thing you will do is decide how big you want the finished quilt to be and that determines how big each unit will be. If you change the "Unit Size", then click inside the "Design Size", box you will see the adjusted design size.

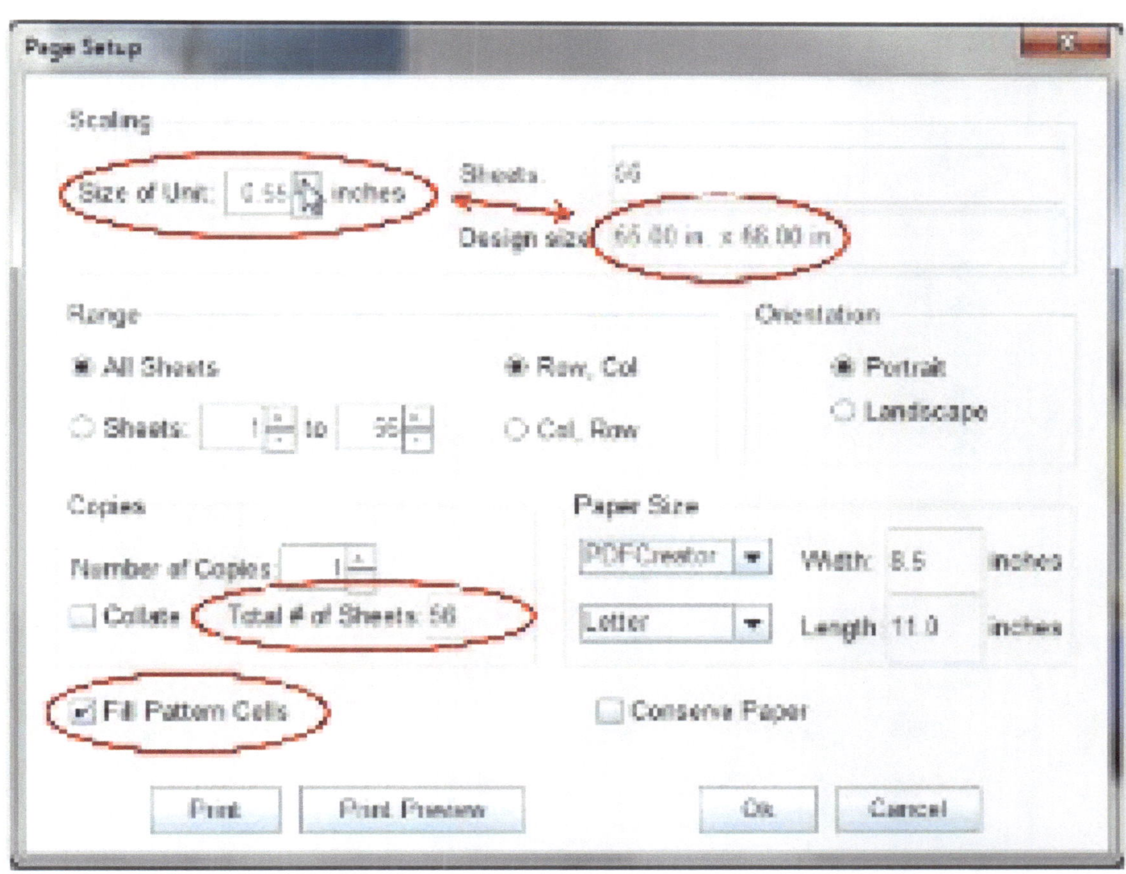

The purpose of adjusting the "Unit Size" is to control the finished size of your quilt.

If you make a large pattern, the larger your "Design Size" is, the more pages your pattern will have because your pattern will be a series of printer pages to create the pattern size of your choice.

The pages are labeled by row and column and you will tape the pages together (it's easy to do).

IMPORTANT: Before you print the pattern, you must click "Fill Pattern Cells" to make a full color pattern.

Now you can see what the pattern will look like. What we're looking for are large areas of color. You will cut straight lines, even though the lines seem to be jagged. You'll draw smooth lines following the color.

In the next chapter, I'll go into detail showing you exactly how to cut out the pattern pieces and the whole process of putting the quilt together. It's actually very easy and very simple. This type of pattern is really simple because you follow the color and not numbers.

I have made a video of this demo and you can see the demo for free because you purchased this book. If you don't already have the software, you can try it out totally free for 7-days. You can also see the video demo when you join the free online course. To get your free gifts, go to page 88 for the details.

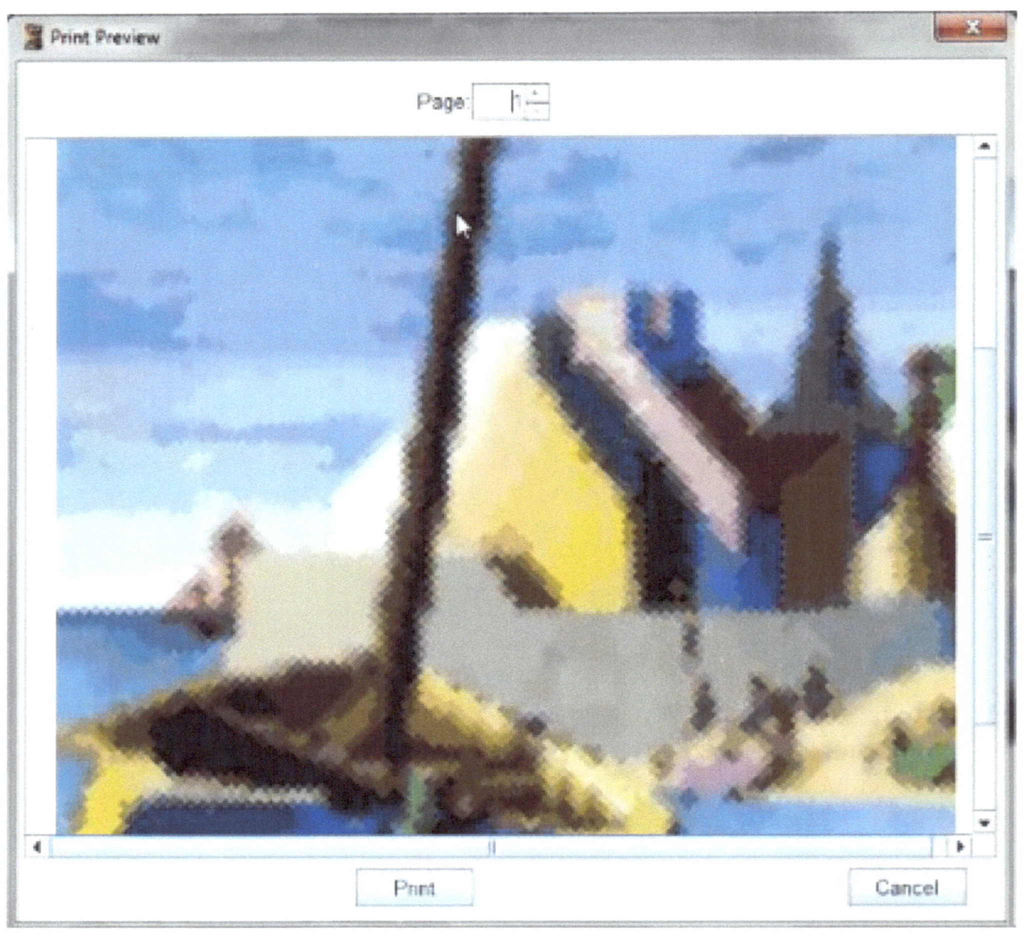

Chapter 3

How To Prepare Your Pattern

I'm going to show you how to prepare your pattern so that you can start your project.

When you print out your pattern according to the instructions in chapter 2, the first thing you'll notice is that it is in full color. You can see (pattern on the previous page) that it's the same colors as the original picture but much larger.

To put the pattern together, notice that the top of each page of the pattern is labeled with the row and column.

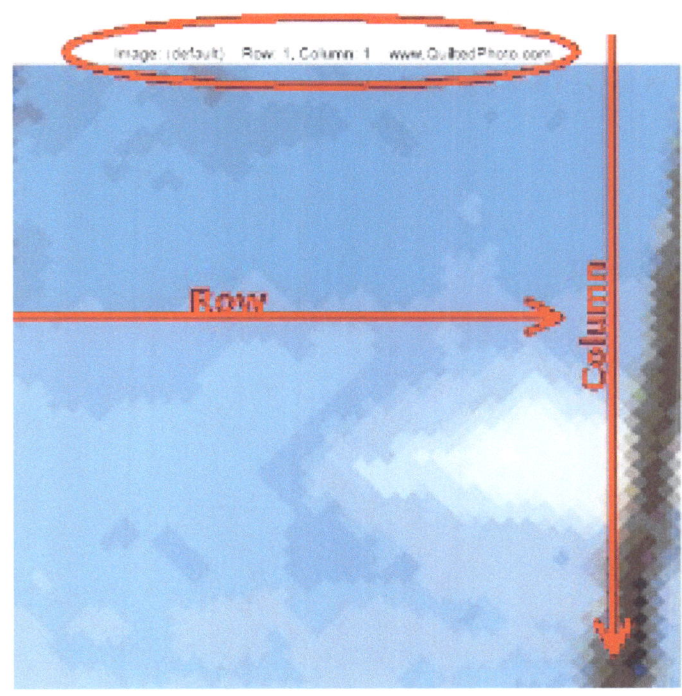

The labels are at the top of each page so that you can put your pattern together in the correct order. Remember that, rows go across and columns go up and down.

I suggest that you put together the columns first because that will make the whole process easier.

Before you tape the pages together, you'll need to cut off the borders on the the pages so you can put the pattern pages together seamlessly. I usually cut off the white border on the left side and bottom edge only. When I say cut off the border, you cut right on the edge of the color, eliminating about 1/4" of paper.

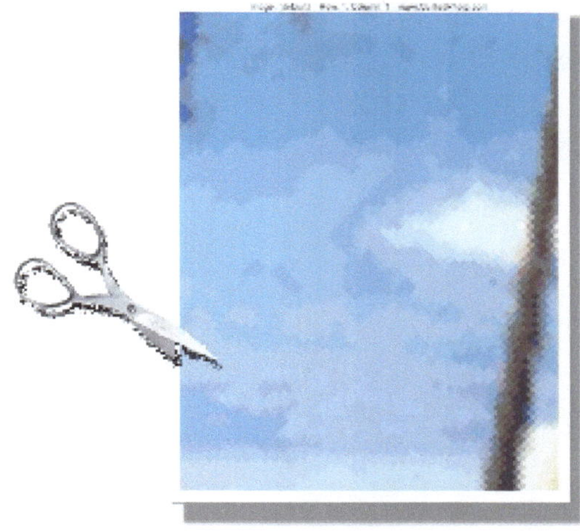

Lay them out in order because you don't want to put your pages out of order.

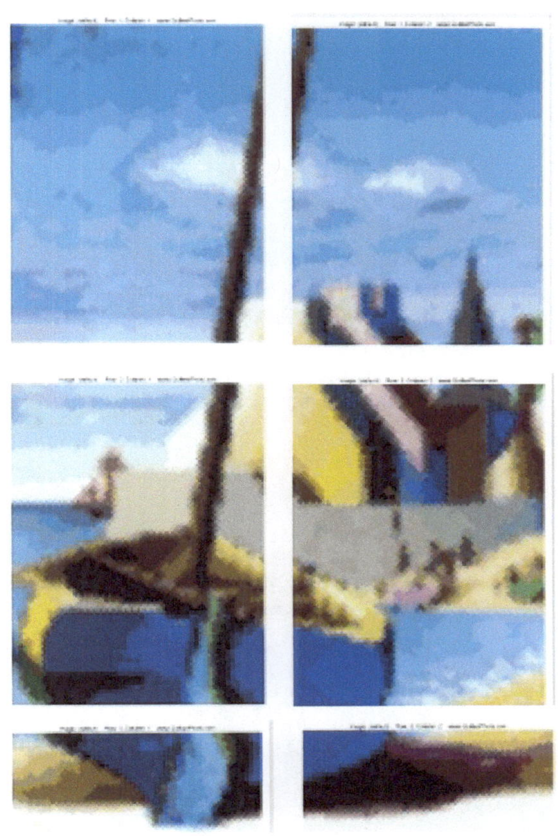

To put the first column together, you'll need to add each page one at a time. Since you've cut off that white border on the bottom of the first page (row 1, column 1), you'll simply place the next page (row 2 column 1) underneath and tape them together. I suggest that you put tape right on top of the page seam. Continue on the same way with each page until the column is complete.

The last step is to simply tape all of the columns together until the whole pattern is completed.

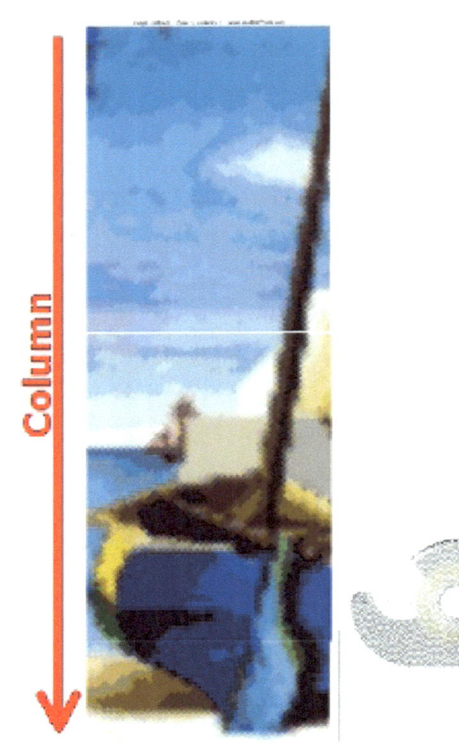

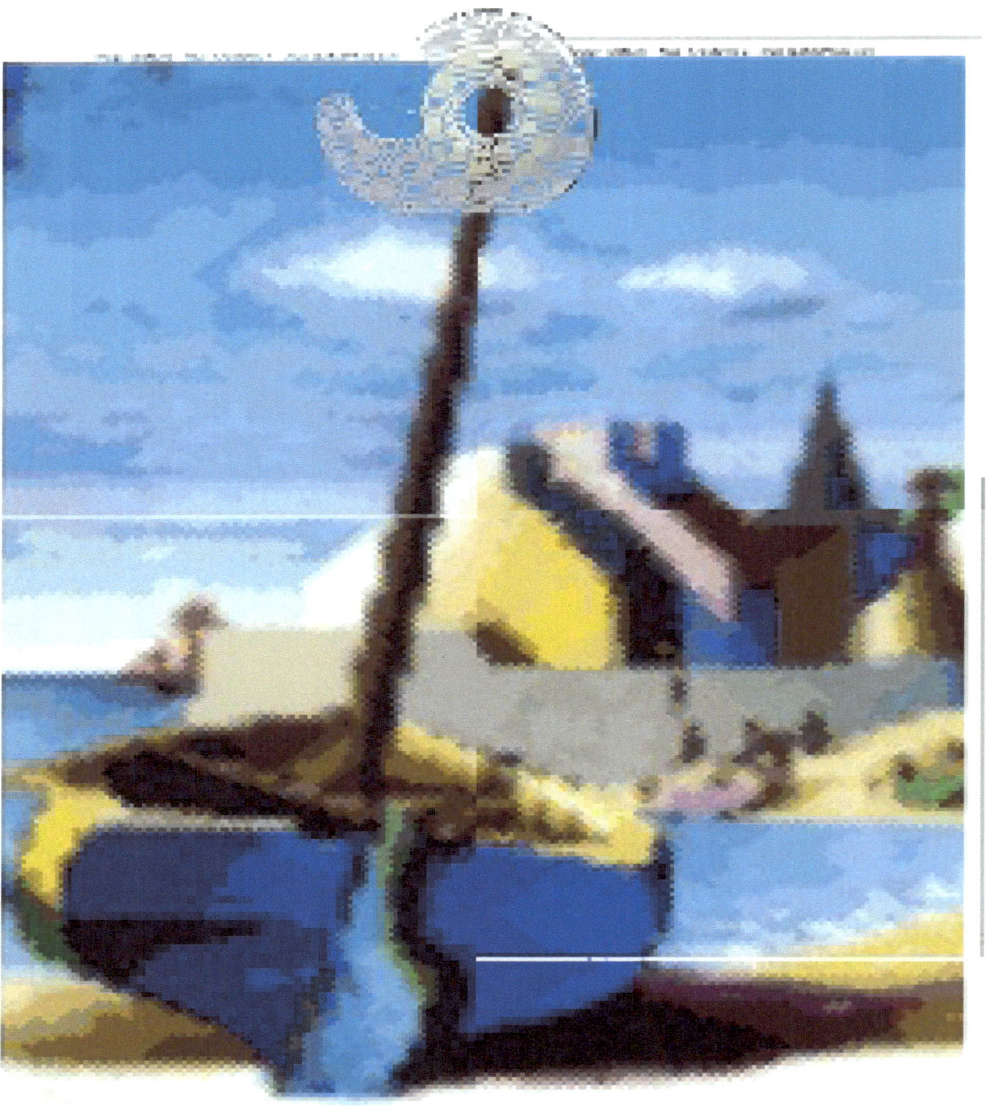

Chapter 4

Essential Tools And Supplies

In the previous chapters I taught you how to choose a picture and how to make the patterns. Now I'm going to talk about the essential tools and the supplies that are very helpful for the techniques in this book.

The first thing you're going to need is some good scissors. I suggest a small pair that has a 2" blade. The kind of scissors that have a spring is also helpful to avoid fatigue in your hands.

Another thing you're going to need for this technique is the "Simply Amazing Quilting Film". This film is going to be an important tool for this technique. It will help with stitching placement and stitching design. "Simply Amazing Quilting Film" is a very useful tool.

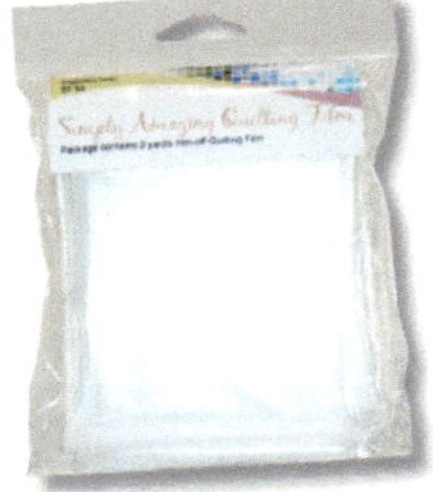

The next item you're going to need is Steam-A-Seam. You can find it in most quilt shops and fabric stores. It is available in sheets and also by the yard. If you decide to use Steam-A-Seam, buy it from the roll because you can get the exact yardage you need. I do not recommend the 'Lite" version of this product.

Instead of using Steam-A-Seam, another option is to make your own sticky web. I use fusible web, parchment paper and basting spray to make it. Look on page 46 for detailed instructions on how to make your own sticky web. I also have prepared a video in the online video course that is included with this book. To get your free online course, go to page 88.

If you decide to make your own sticky web, you will need parchment paper. You can find parchment paper in most grocery stores in the baking section alongside the aluminum foil and the plastic wrap.

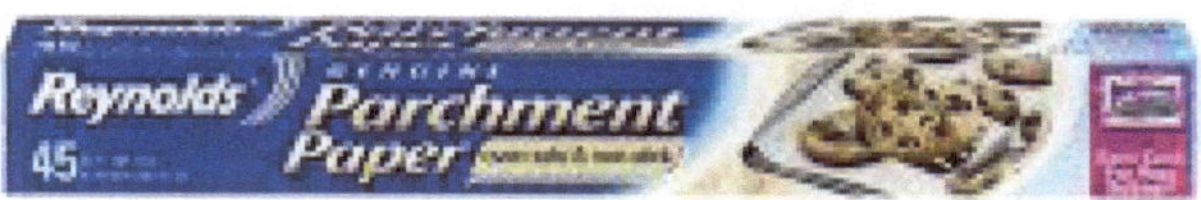

Quilt basting spray is also needed to make your own sticky web. It can be easily found at quilt shops and online.

The good thing about making it yourself is that you can create large pieces of sticky web and it comes out much more affordable than buying Steam-A-Seam.

You can use any fusible web you want, but I offer extra wide fusible web at a great price in my online store and it comes in 60 inches wide x 2 yard pieces. The retail stores only offer fusible web yardage 20 inches wide.

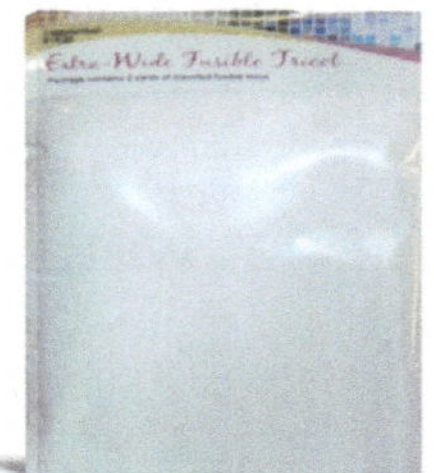

Another item you can use is "Fusible Tricot". You would use this only if you're going to make a large size quilt (see chapter 7). If you want to make a quilt that will remain soft like a blanket, you should use the fusible tricot.

How To Make Your Own Sticky Web

Here are the items you'll need:

1. Parchment Paper
2. Fusible Web
3. Basting Spray / Craft adhesive spray
4. Stapler - You can use a normal stapler.

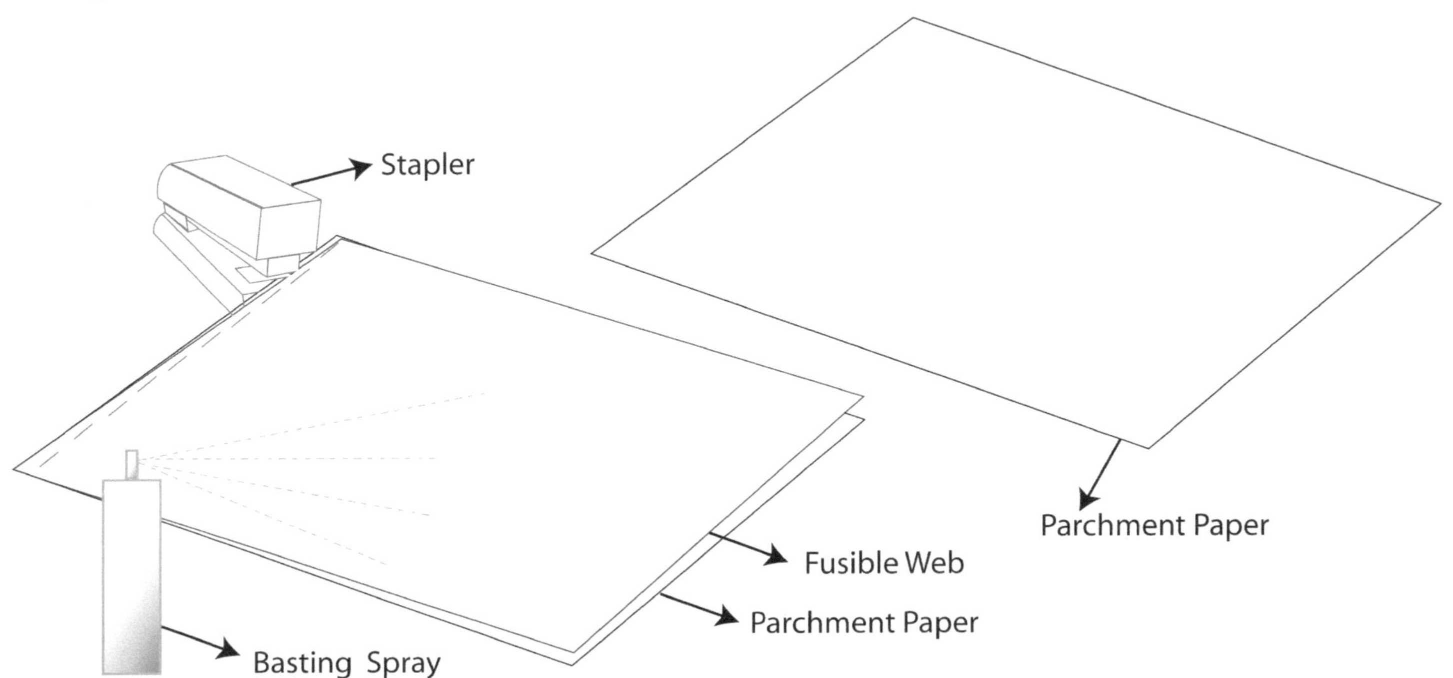

Instructions:

A. Cut a sheet of parchment paper a couple of inches bigger than your pattern (you can staple two sheets of parchment paper together to make a large sheet if necessary).

B. Cut a piece of Fusible Web to match the size of the parchment paper. Staple the top edge of the parchment and fusible web as shown in the image above. You can also staple the bottom edge to keep the layers from moving around.

C. Spray the top of the fusible web with the basting spray. Allow to dry. It should be sticky but not wet. Spray a second layer of basting spray and allow it to dry for a few more minutes.

Now is the time to touch the fusible web with a small piece of fabric to make sure it is sticky enough to hold the fabric securely. If the fabric is not holding securely, spray with another layer of basting spray.

D. To finish your home made sticky web, add another sheet of parchment paper on the top.

Chapter 5

Fabric and Thread Choices

In this chapter I'm going to talk about fabric choices, as well as thread choices. They are both very important.

In chapter 1 and 2 you were instructed how to choose a picture with only a few colors, but just because you're using just a few colors, it doesn't mean that you must choose only one fabric choice per color. You can choose several fabrics of each color. For example, if you want to use pink or fuchsia, you should use several different pink or fuchsia fabrics. The picture below is one representation of fabrics you could choose for your project.

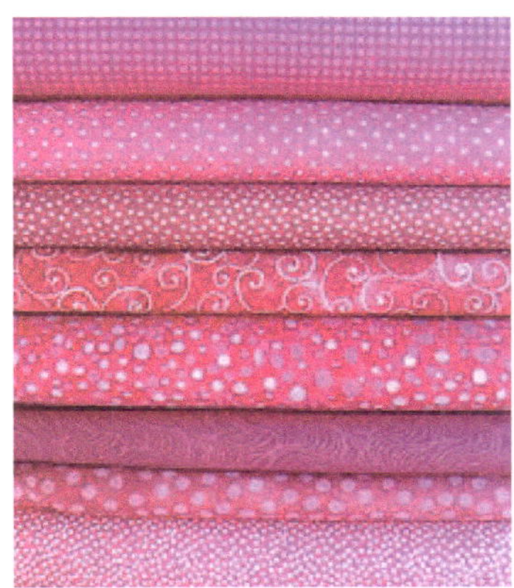

If you have blue in your picture, you can choose several blue fabrics like in the picture below. I really like batiks and jelly rolls. They are perfect because they usually offer a useful range of colors.

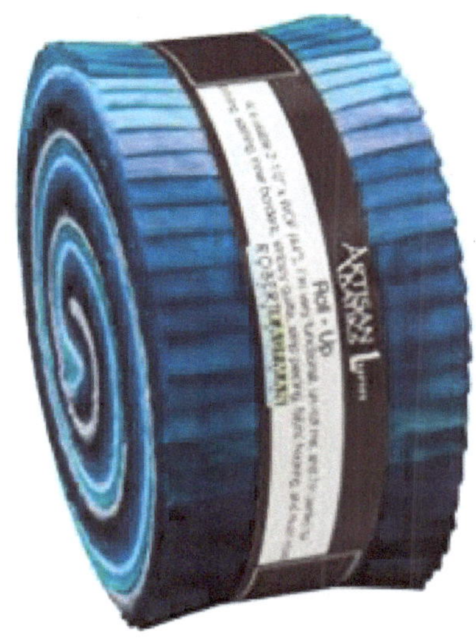

When there is a large area of one color on your quilt, divide the area into smaller sections and use the array of fabrics you've chosen for that color. The key is to make sure the same fabric is never next to itself in the adjoining sections.

The quilt below is a great example of how to use several different fabrics in one larger area. Look at the blue background and notice the many fabrics but they still appear as one blue background. The canopy of the tree is also done the same way (several pale orange/pink fabrics). Using an assortment of fabrics for each

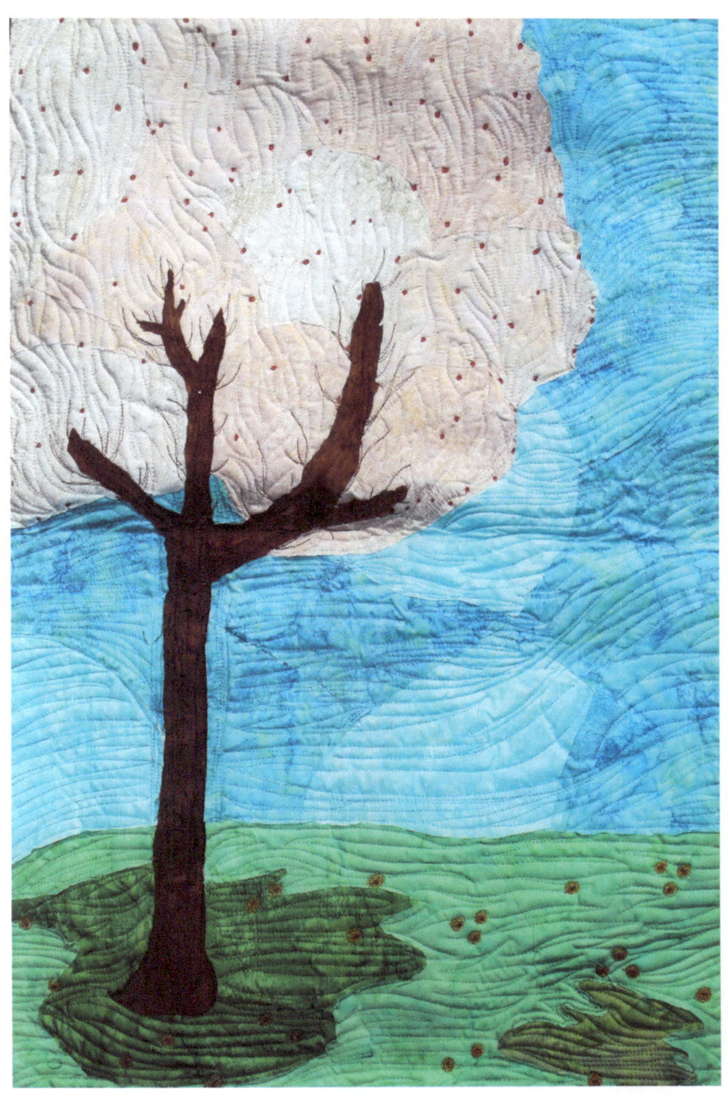

color makes the quilt more exciting and beautiful to look at.

Now I'm going to talk about thread. The big thing that I look for when I'm choosing thread is that it must have one range of color only. We are using a small number of fabric colors, so we only need one varigated spool of thread for each of the fabric colors. I really like variegated threads, but the variegated threads must have only one range of color.

These are good examples of the type of thread I would use. They contain many different shades of the same color. We're going to stitch right on top of the fabrics with the same color. The spool below has green and red colors in the same thread. This would not work well because the red would stand out when stitching on green fabric and the green would stand out when stitching on red fabric.

Most of the time I recommend that you match the thread and fabric colors but there is a time to use contrasting thread. That is when you want to make a detail more visible or you want to make a detail stand out from the rest of the picture. A good example of using contrasting thread is when you stitch the signature of the artist on the quilt. You can see an example of this on the quilt below.

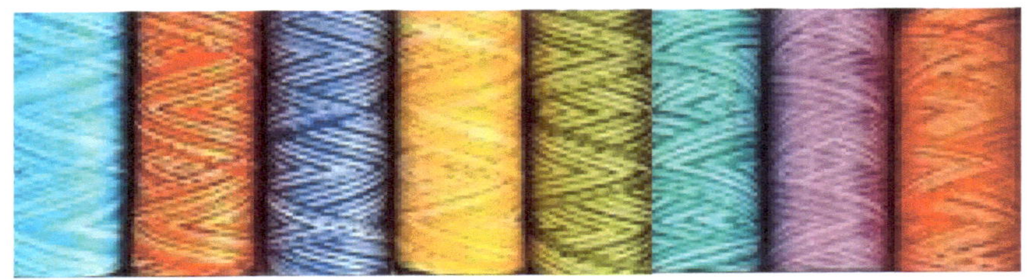

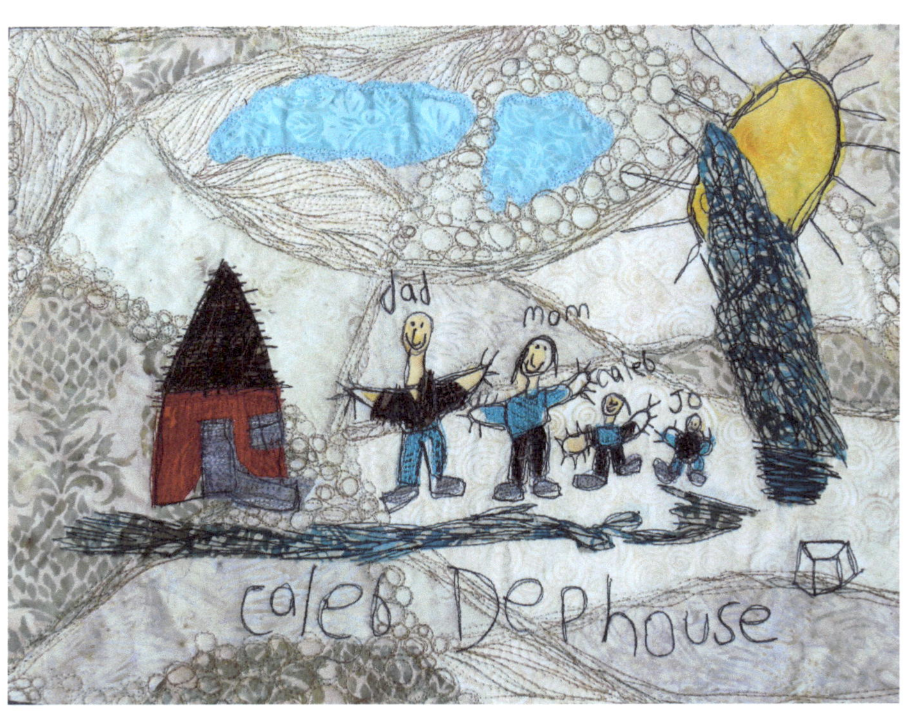

Chapter 6

Putting The Quilt Together - Technique 1

We're going to talk about putting the quilt together. This technique is best used for making art quilts to hang on the wall.

A. To get started, peel the back parchment paper off of your sticky web or Steam-A-Seam. Leave the top sheet of parchment paper in place.

B. Place your Pattern on the table.

C. Then place your sticky web (or Steam-A-Seam) on top of your pattern keeping the top parchment paper in place. Put a couple of pins in the two upper corners to keep the pattern in place.

You will be able to clearly see your color pattern right through your parchment paper and sticky web.

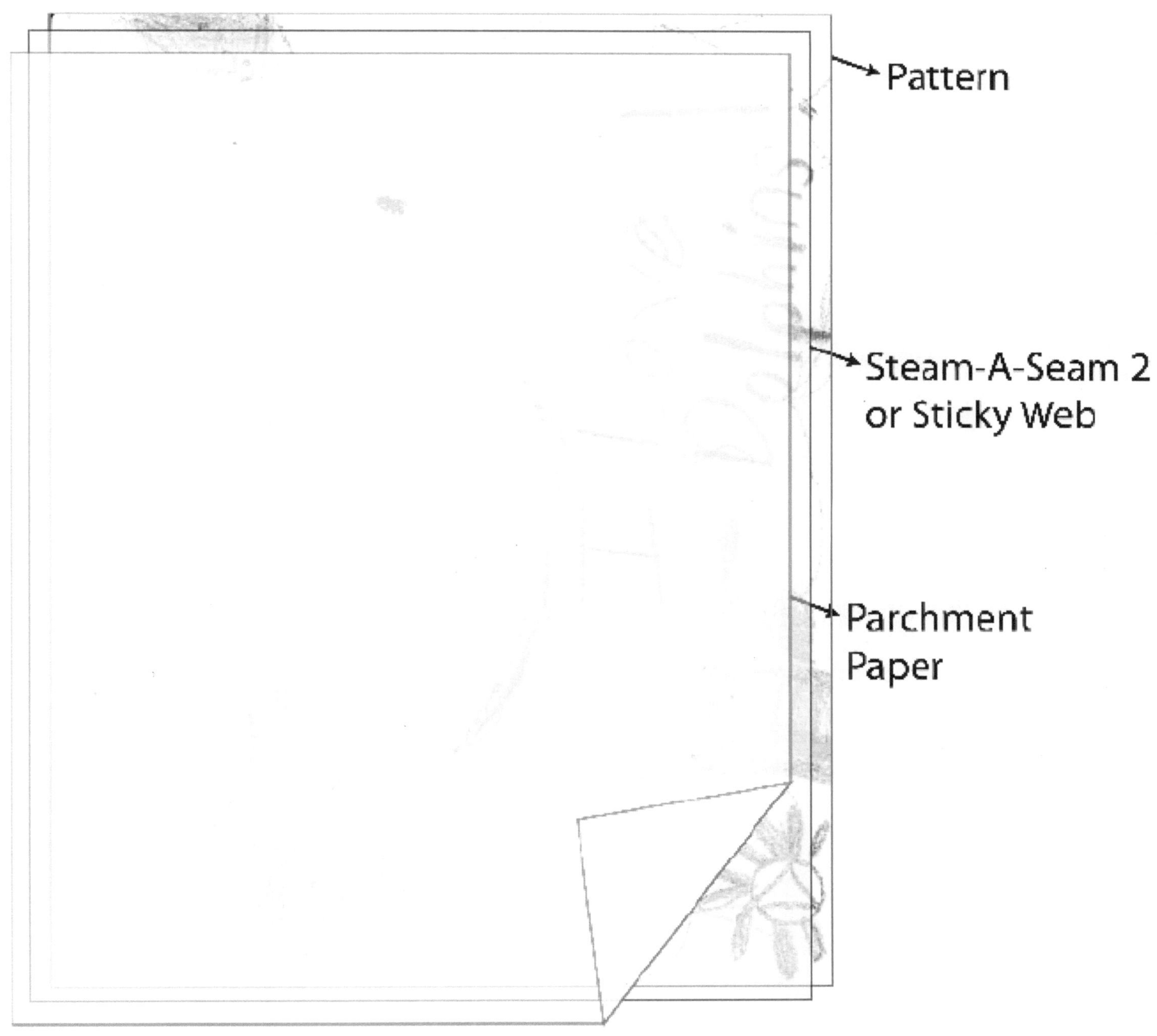

D. Make sure that the sticky surface of the web is facing up (not sticking to your paper pattern). When you fold back the parchment paper on the top, it should be sticky because you need the sticky layer to hold down your fabric pieces later.

E. Use a pencil to trace the first contoured shape onto the top parchment paper. Choose a shape that is next to the edge of the pattern. You'll be able to see the colors through the parchment paper. What we're trying to do is section off the colored pieces on the paper.

I've had some people ask, "Should I cut all the same color pieces at once?" and my answer to that is no. You start from one side and then you will just do whatever comes next because you need all of the paper for the pattern pieces.

In the online video course, I've included some advance tips and you are invited to join the course for free because you purchased this book! To get your free online course go to page 88.

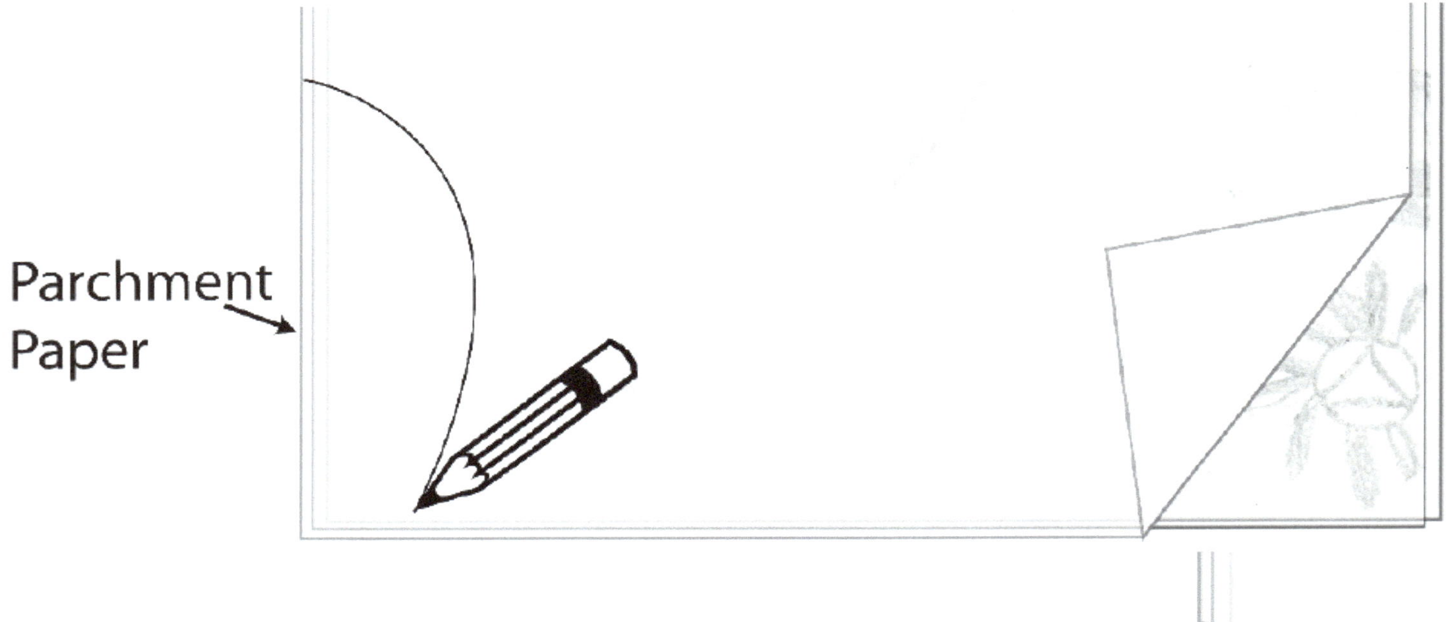

With your pencil, make an outline of an area, following the color. Remember, we're not following pixels. We're following the color.

F. Lift up the edge of the parchment paper and cut out the shape. IMPORTANT: ONLY CUT THE PAPER. NEVER CUT THE STICKY WEB! The paper shape is your pattern piece. You now have an open space exposing the sticky web. This open space is the exact placement for the fabric piece.

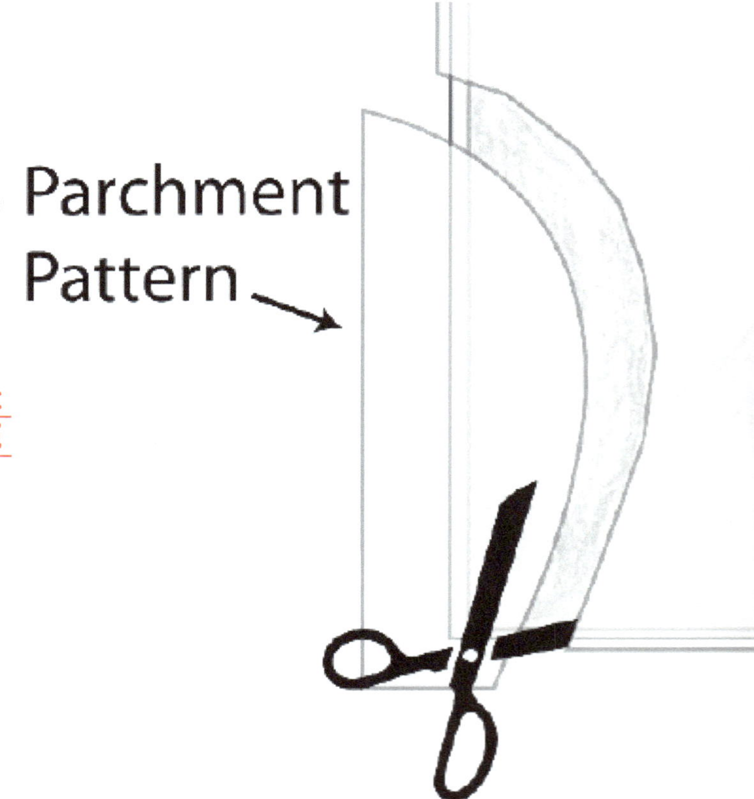

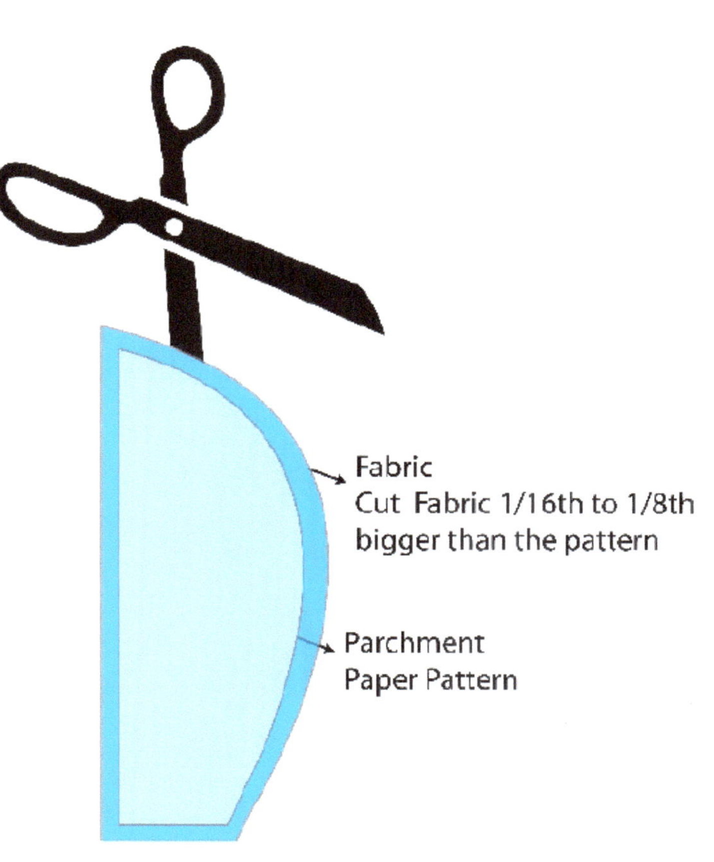

G. Use the paper piece you cut away as your pattern. Match the exposed space on the pattern with the matching fabric. Cut the fabric a little bigger than the pattern (about 1/16th to 1/8th on all sides). You can put a couple of straight pins in there if you can't hold it with your hands. If it's a weird shape and it's moving around, just put a couple of straight pins so it doesn't move. Then cut out your fabric with the right side up. Alternately, you can use several fabrics of the same color to fill in the shape.

H. Discard the paper pattern piece then place the cut fabric on the sticky web with the front side of the fabric facing up. Continue cutting paper pieces one at a time until the whole picture is finished.

I. To finish, remove pins and the paper pattern off the back, and place the whole quilt top directly on your batting and iron the whole thing down.

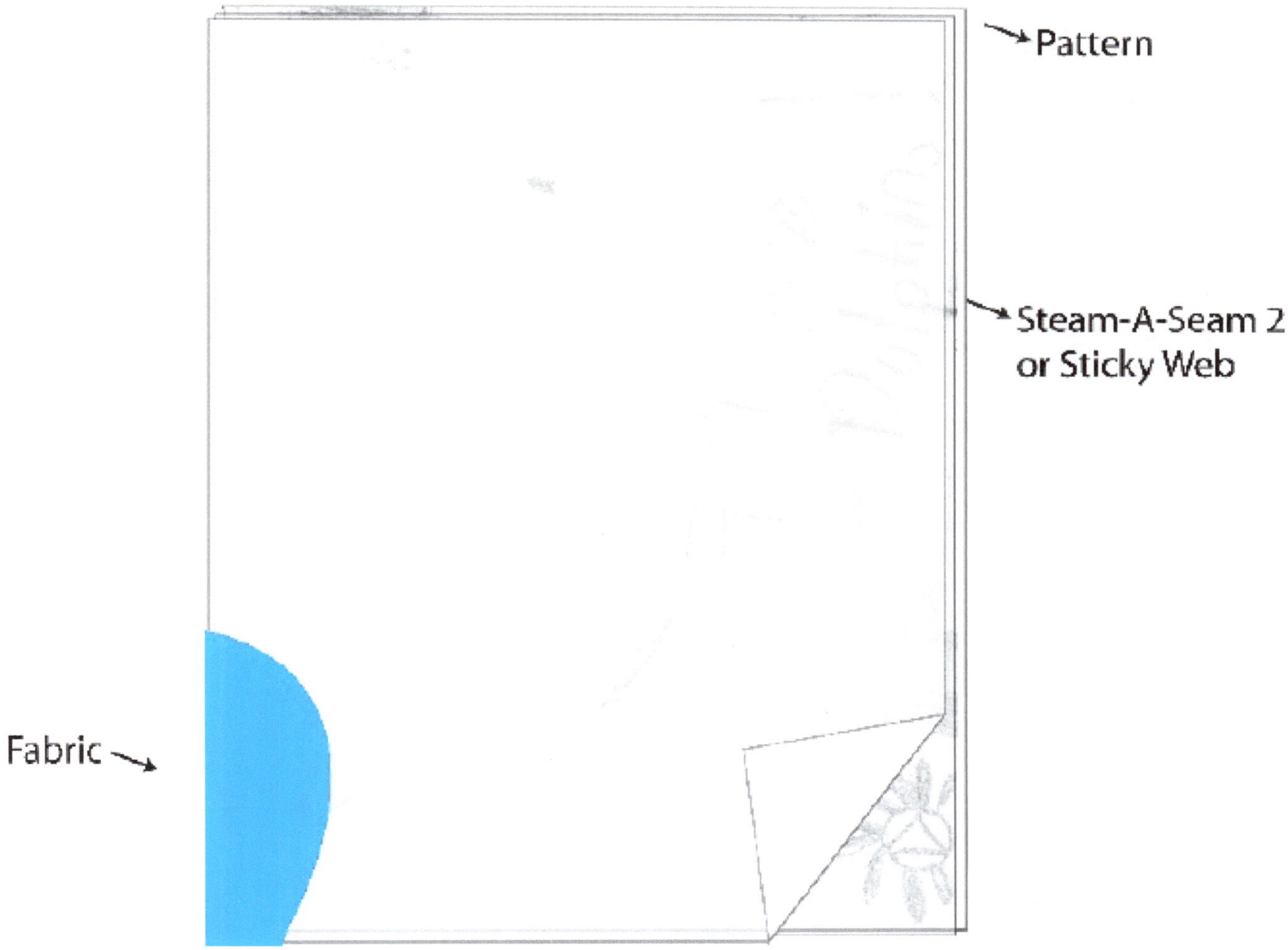

Pattern

Steam-A-Seam 2
or Sticky Web

Fabric

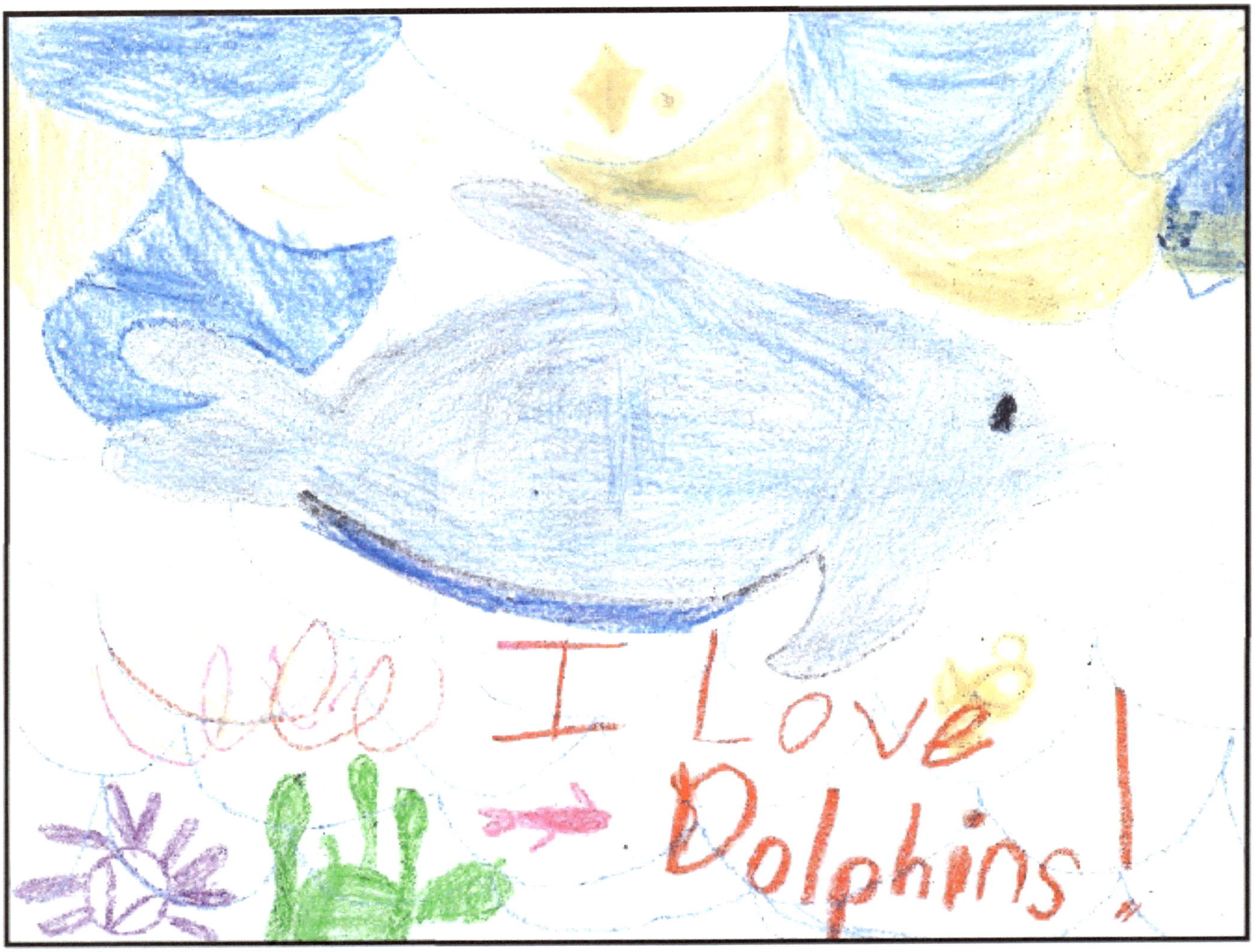

That will make all of your pieces fuse directly to the batting and they will not move around anymore.

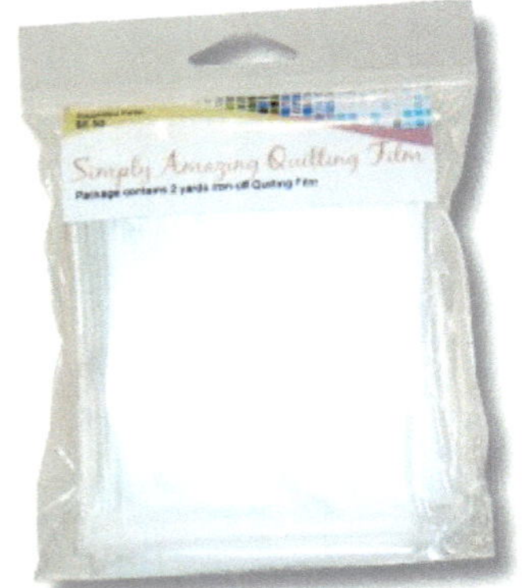

How To Use Quilting Film

To prepare for the stitching, you first place the paper pattern on the table.

J. Place the clear Quilting Film on top of the paper pattern. Pin the Quilting Film so it won't move.

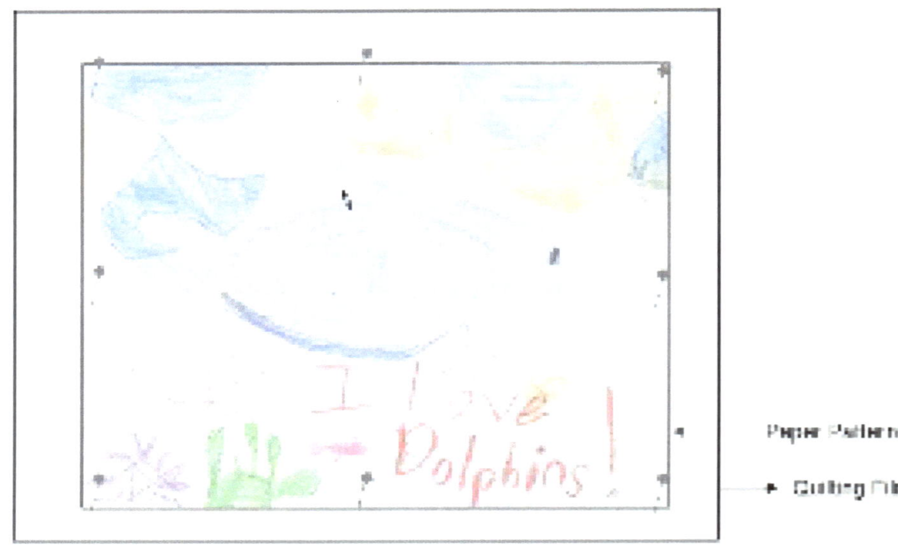

Use a permanent marker to trace the stitching/quilting details onto the film. You can mark all of the stitching or just the top layer of words and scribbles.

In Chapter 2, we talked about layers. In this drawing, the words and little squiggles would be the top layer. Draw all of the details following the pattern. Trace them exactly as they are on the drawing. You may want to mark where the edges and corners of the pattern are too so you can place the film in the correct location on the quilt.

K. Now is the time to stitch the main areas of the picture. Stitch all areas that do not require the quilting film map.

Before you move on to the next step, you should have the whole quilt stitched except for the top layer (writing or signatures etc.) of stitching.

L. Now is the time to use the quilting film that is marked with the top layer of stitching. This film has exact placement of the stitching and will serve as your stitching guide.

Before you do the stitching, use basting spray or a glue stick to secure the film onto the quilt in the proper place. To use the spray, first spray the back side of the film and wait a few moments to let it dry a bit It will get tacky Place the film on top of the quilt. Then go ahead and stitch the top layer of squiggles, details and signature.

After you have finished stitching the top layer of details (as well as your signature) you can tear away all of the excess quilting film that has not been stitched.

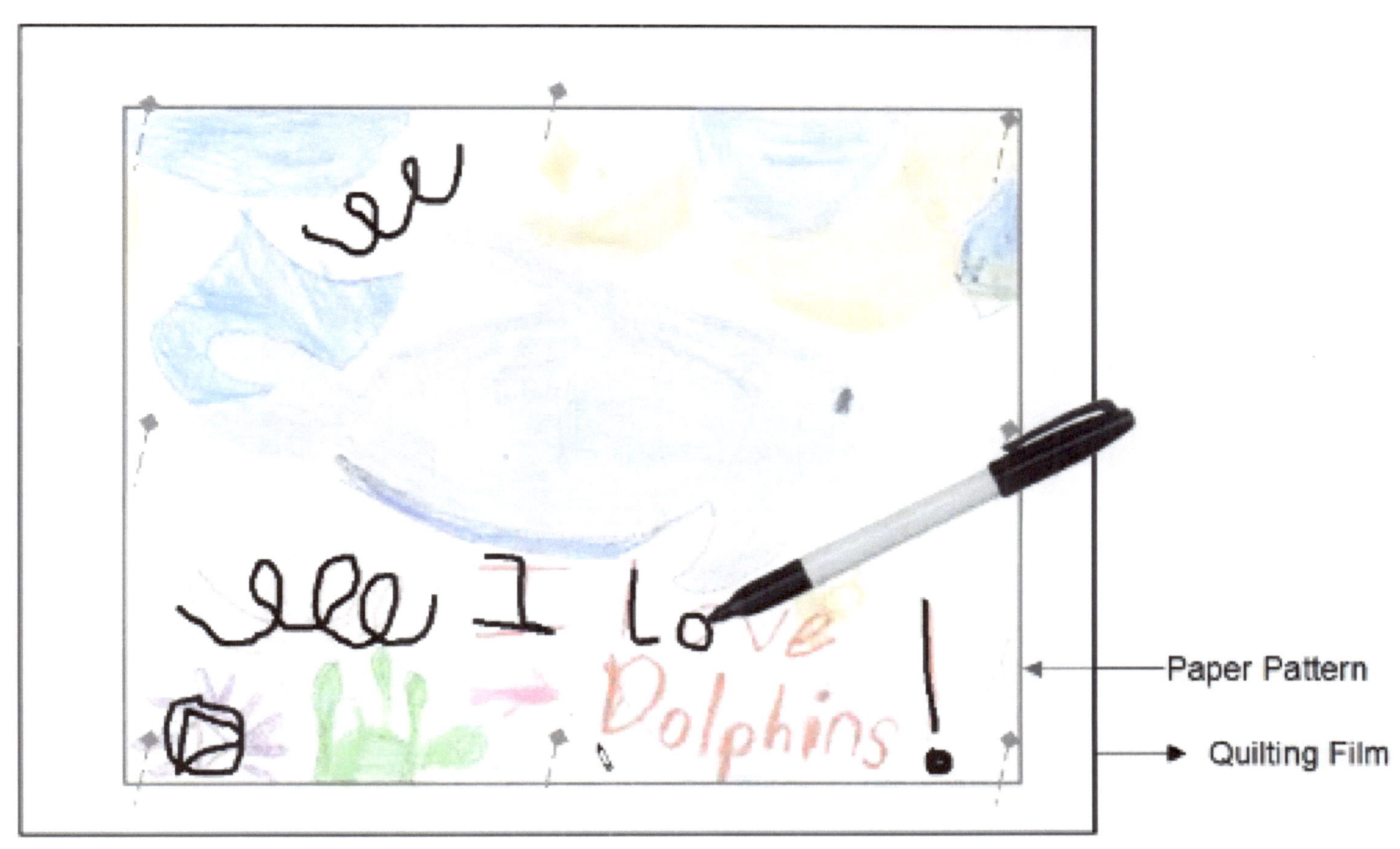

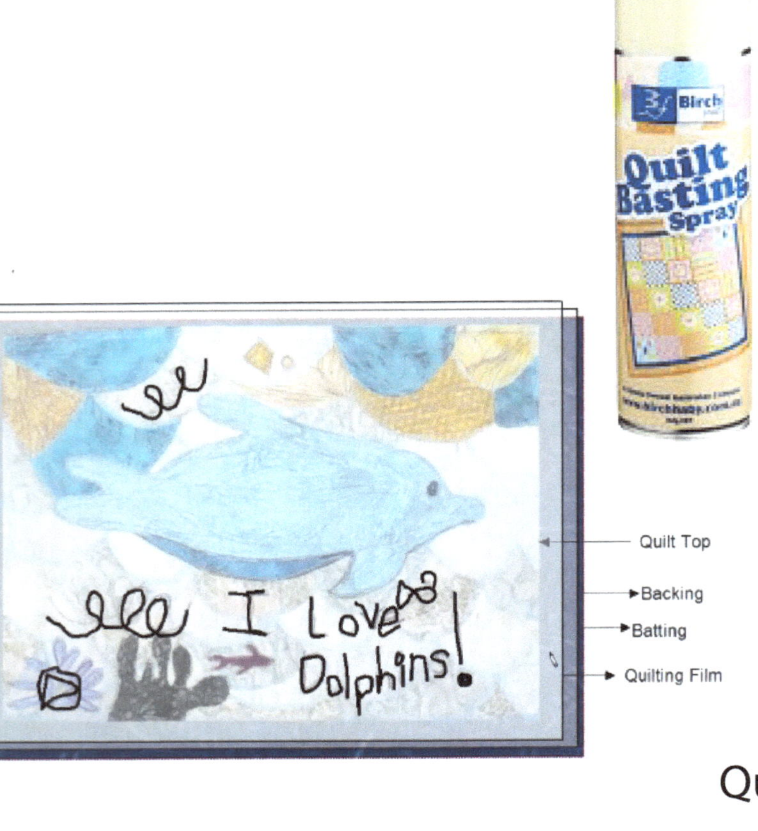

M. The next step is to iron off the remaining bits of quilting film with a very hot iron. Apply a lot of pressure while ironing the film in a circular motion. The film will roll off in little bits. Keep ironing until all of the film is gone. The film will not stick to the iron. This quilting film is a fabulous tool to make quilting your art quilt accurate and easy.

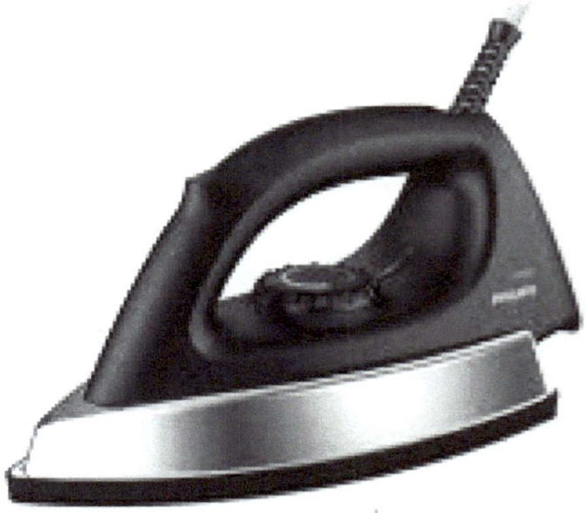

Quilting Film

Quilt

"I Love Dolphins!"
Original art made by
Mikala Toshima

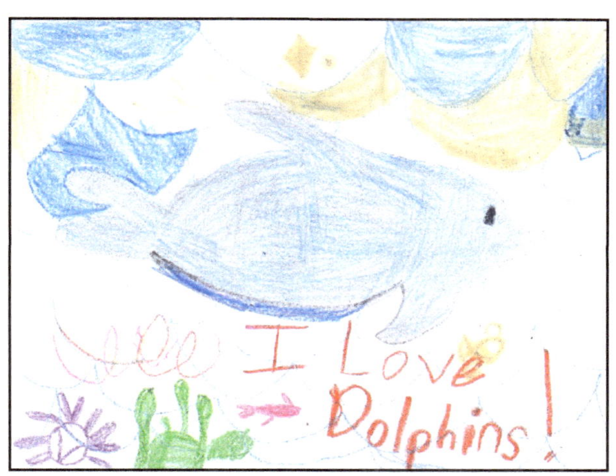

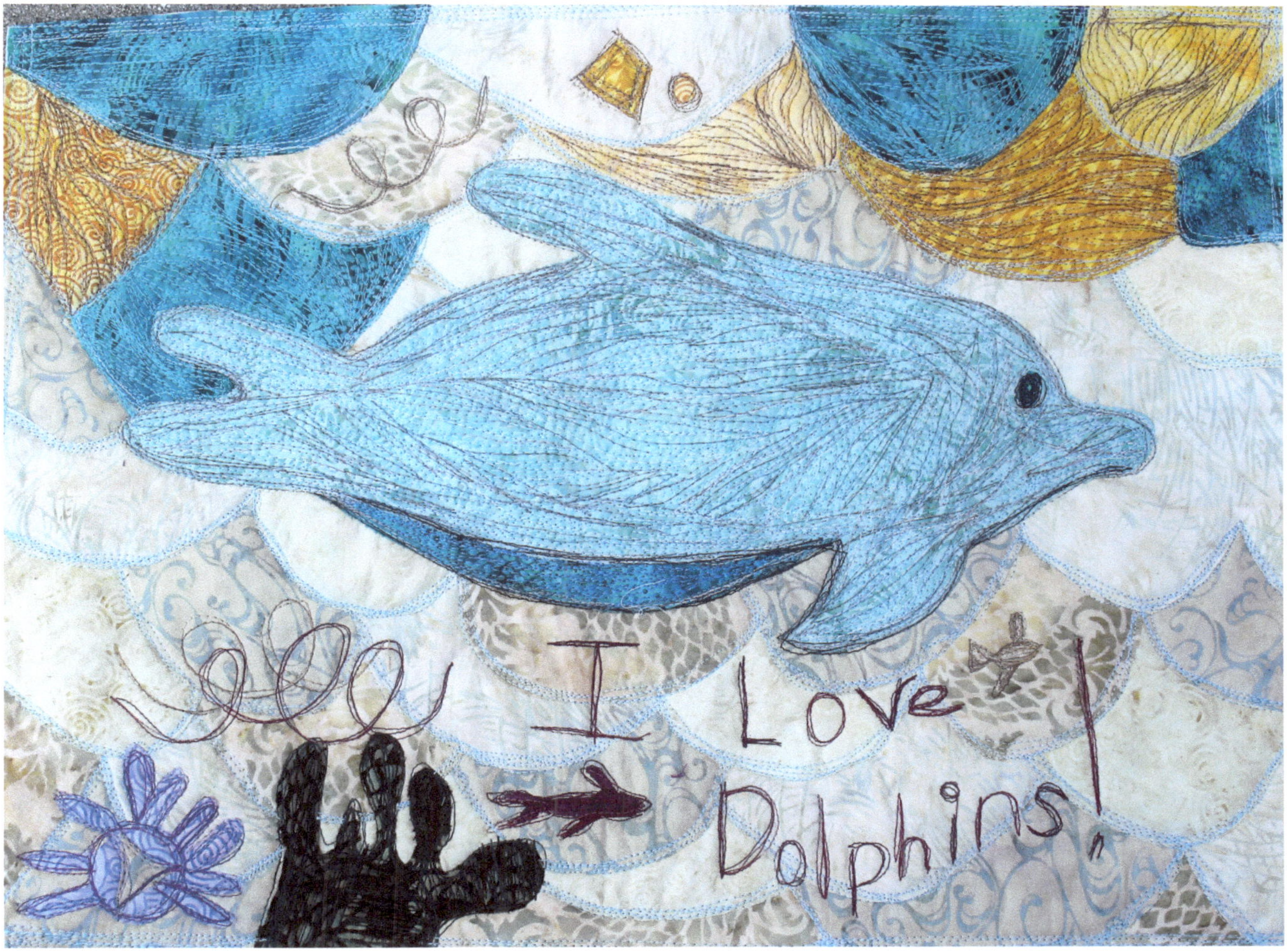

"Dephouse Family Portrait"

Original art made by

Caleb Dephouse

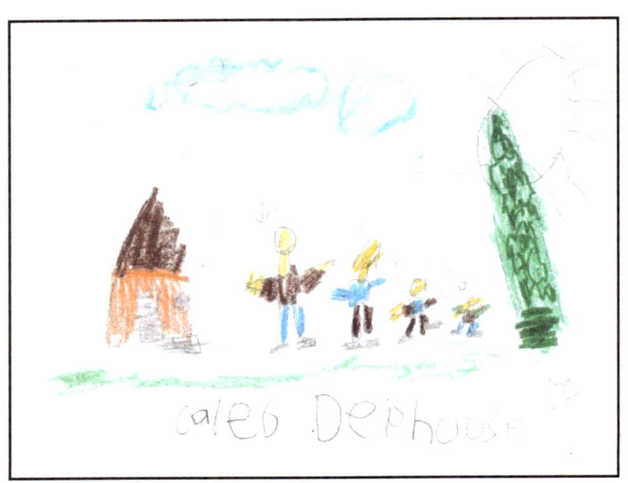

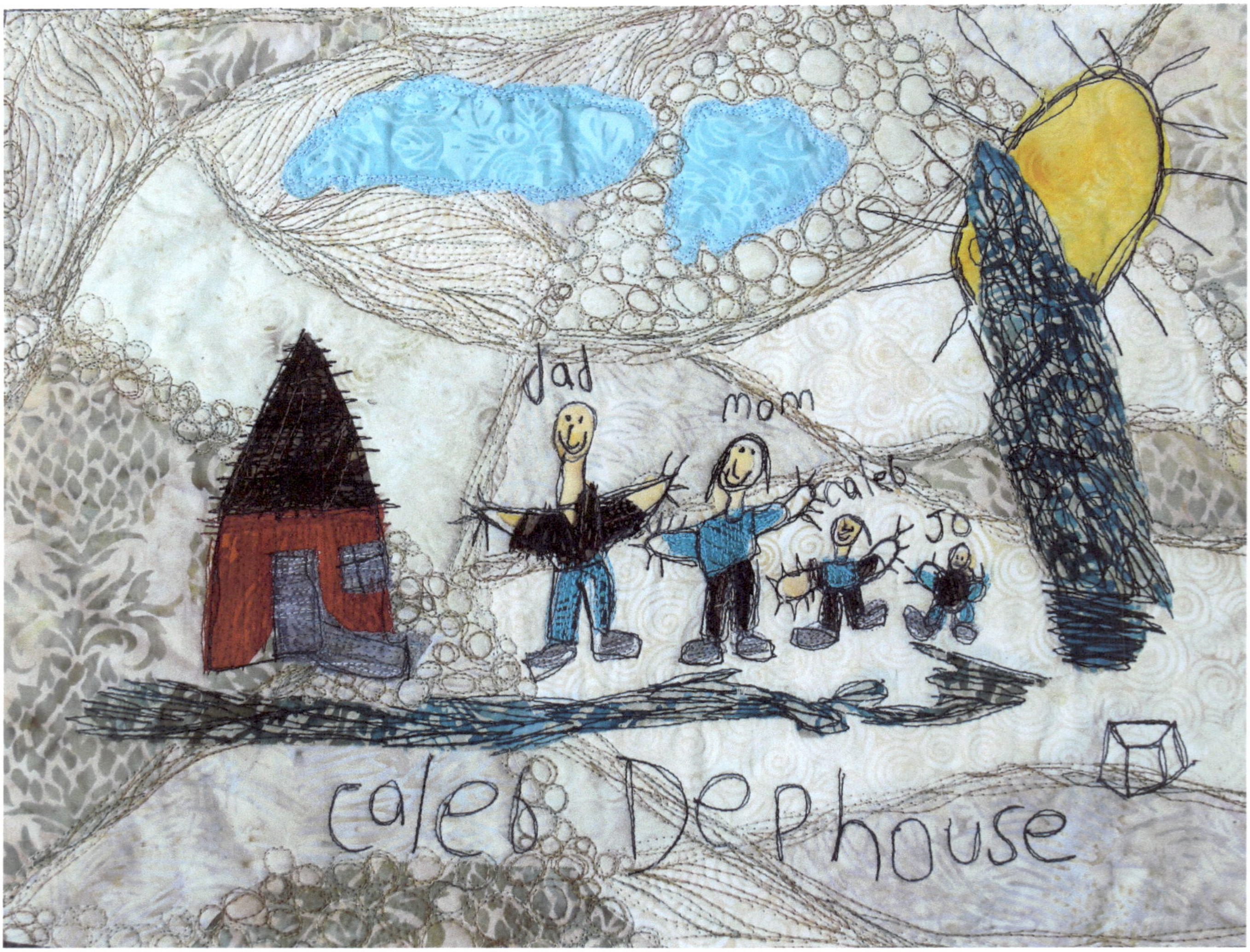

"Natalee, Caleb and Africa"

Original art made by

Kyle Waclaw

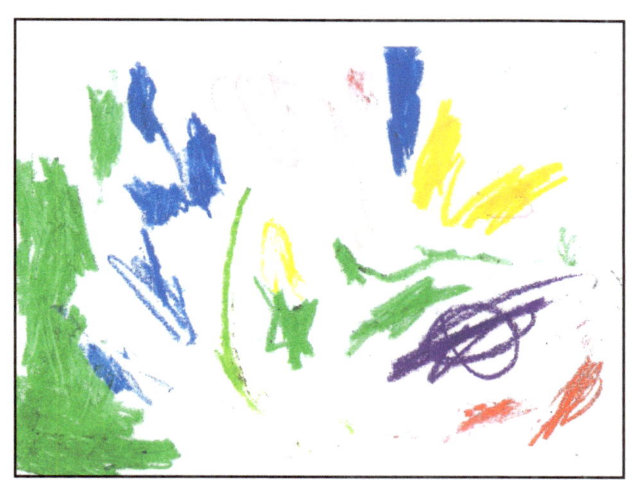

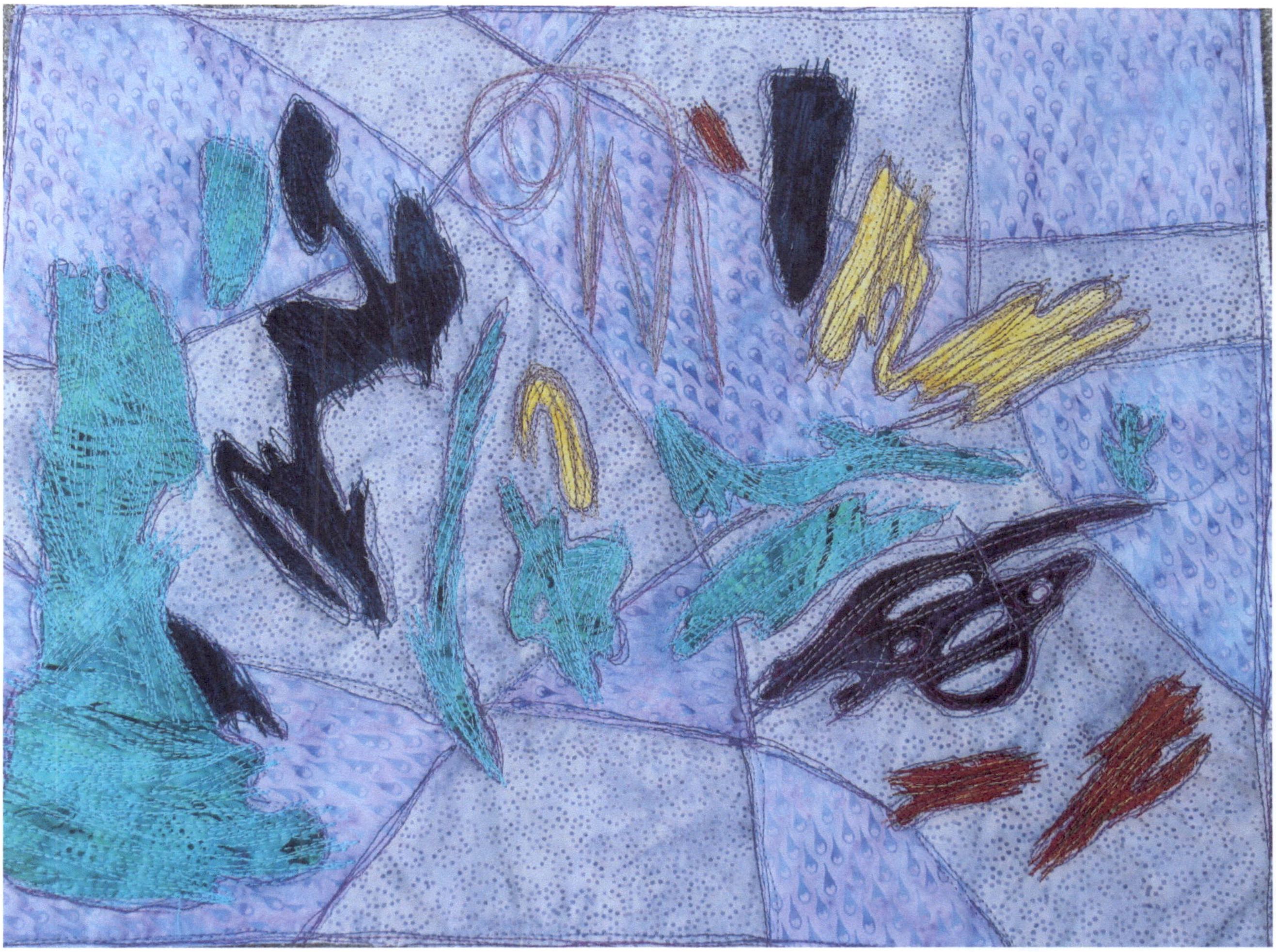

“My House, My Mom and Me”

Original art made by

Anthony Waclaw

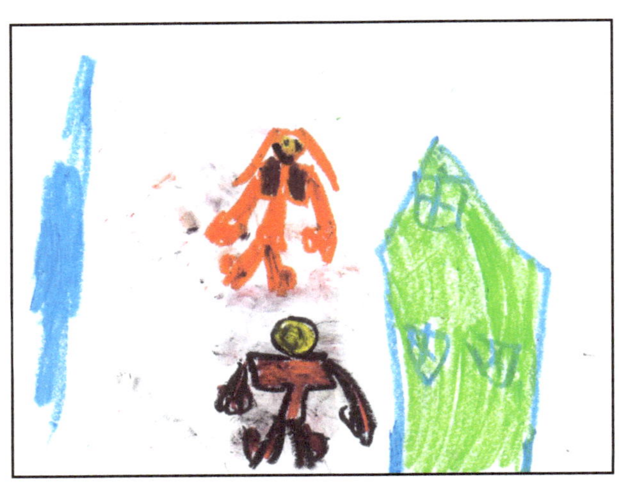

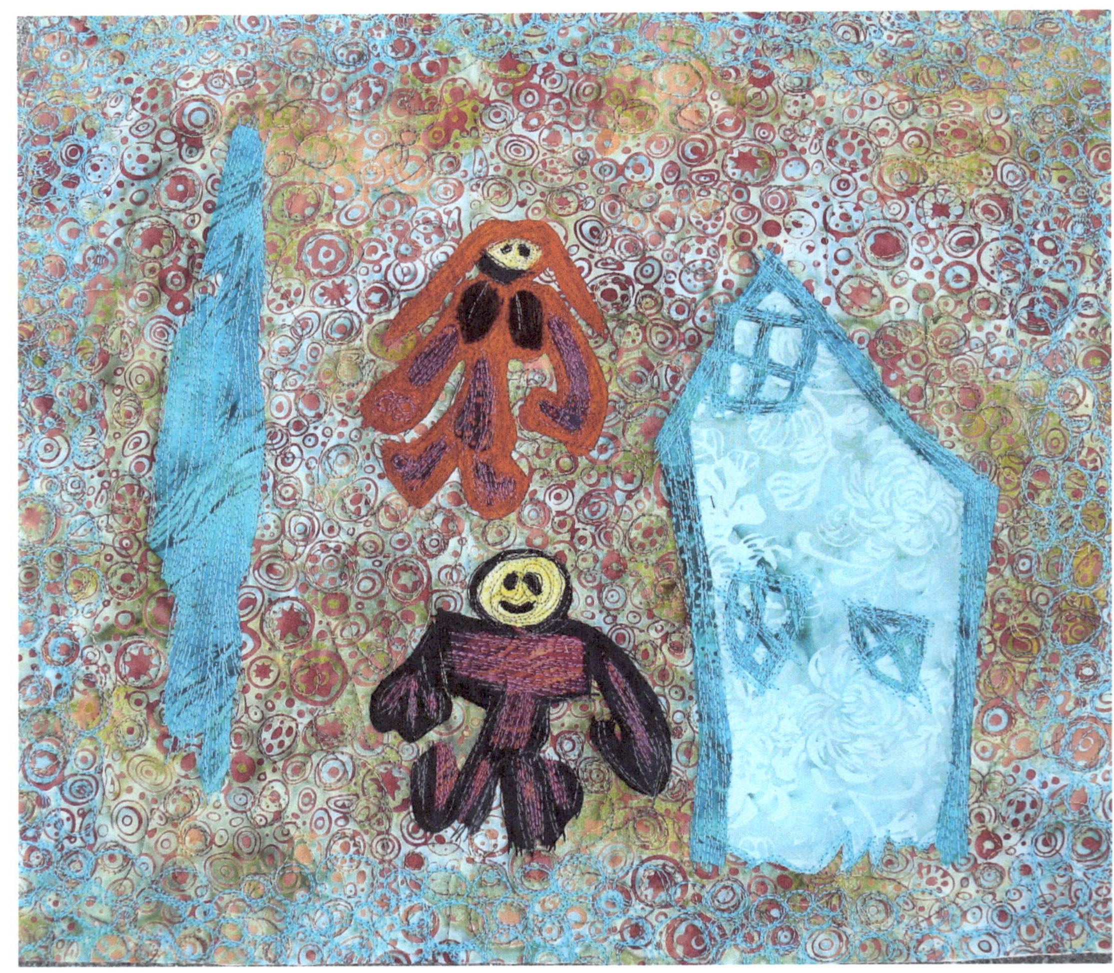

"I Like To Draw Nature"

Original art made by

Brady McMains

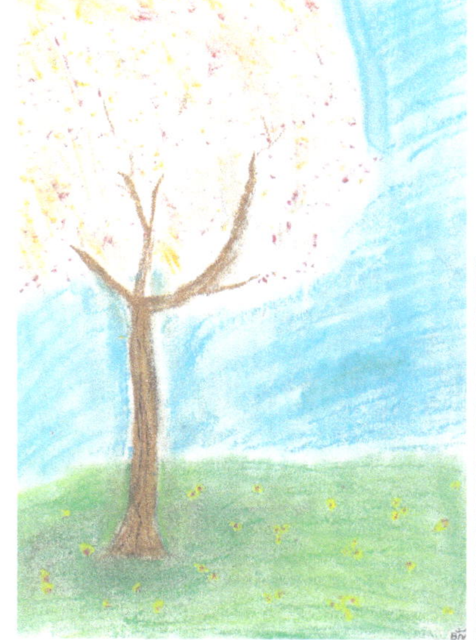

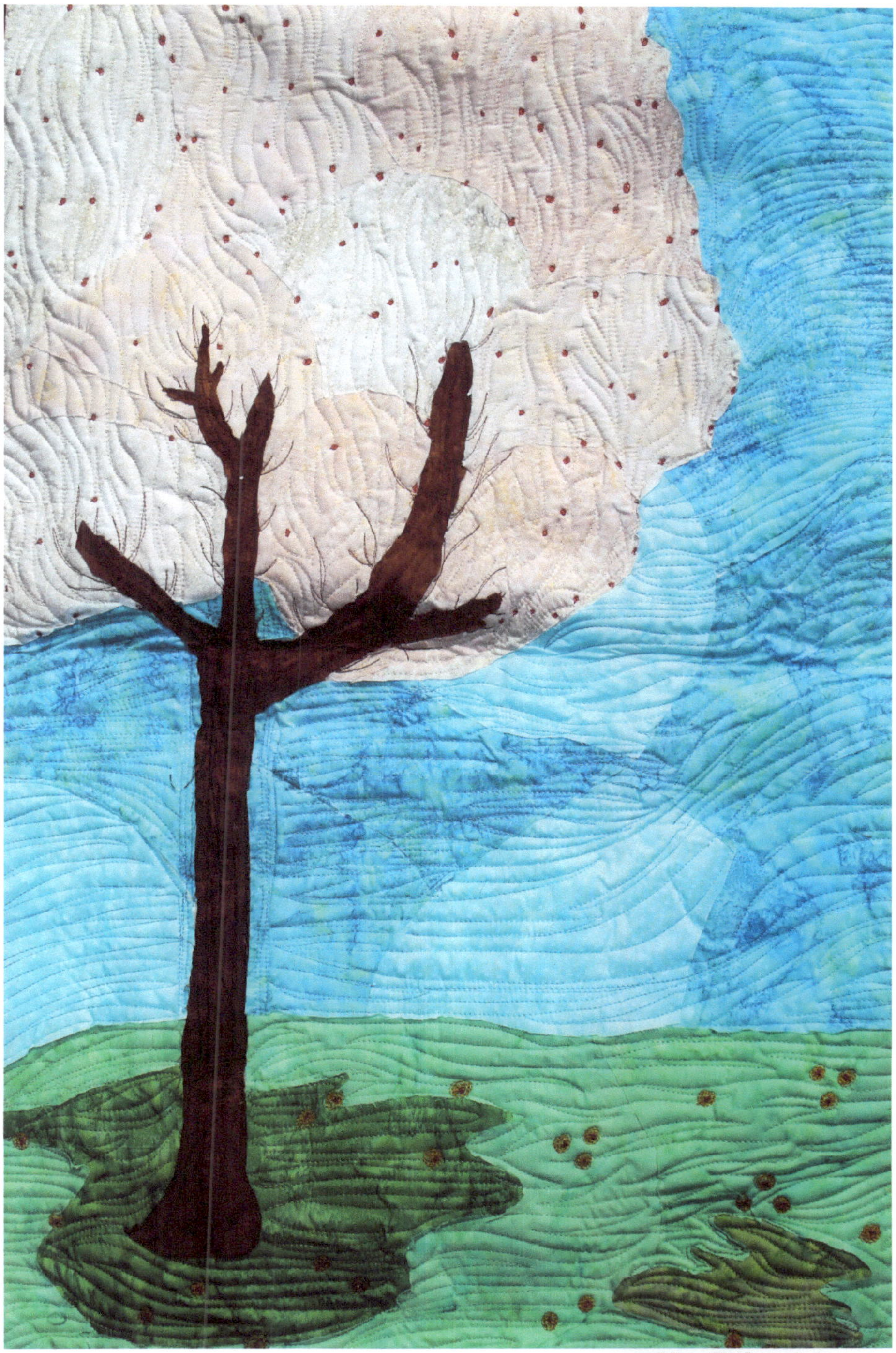

"Mommy and Me"

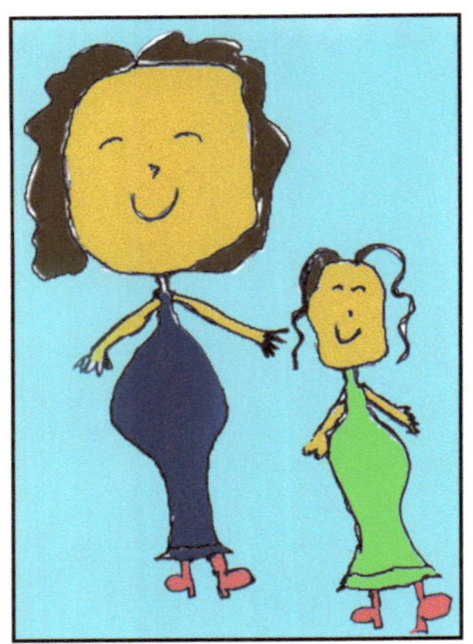

Original art made by

Angela joyner

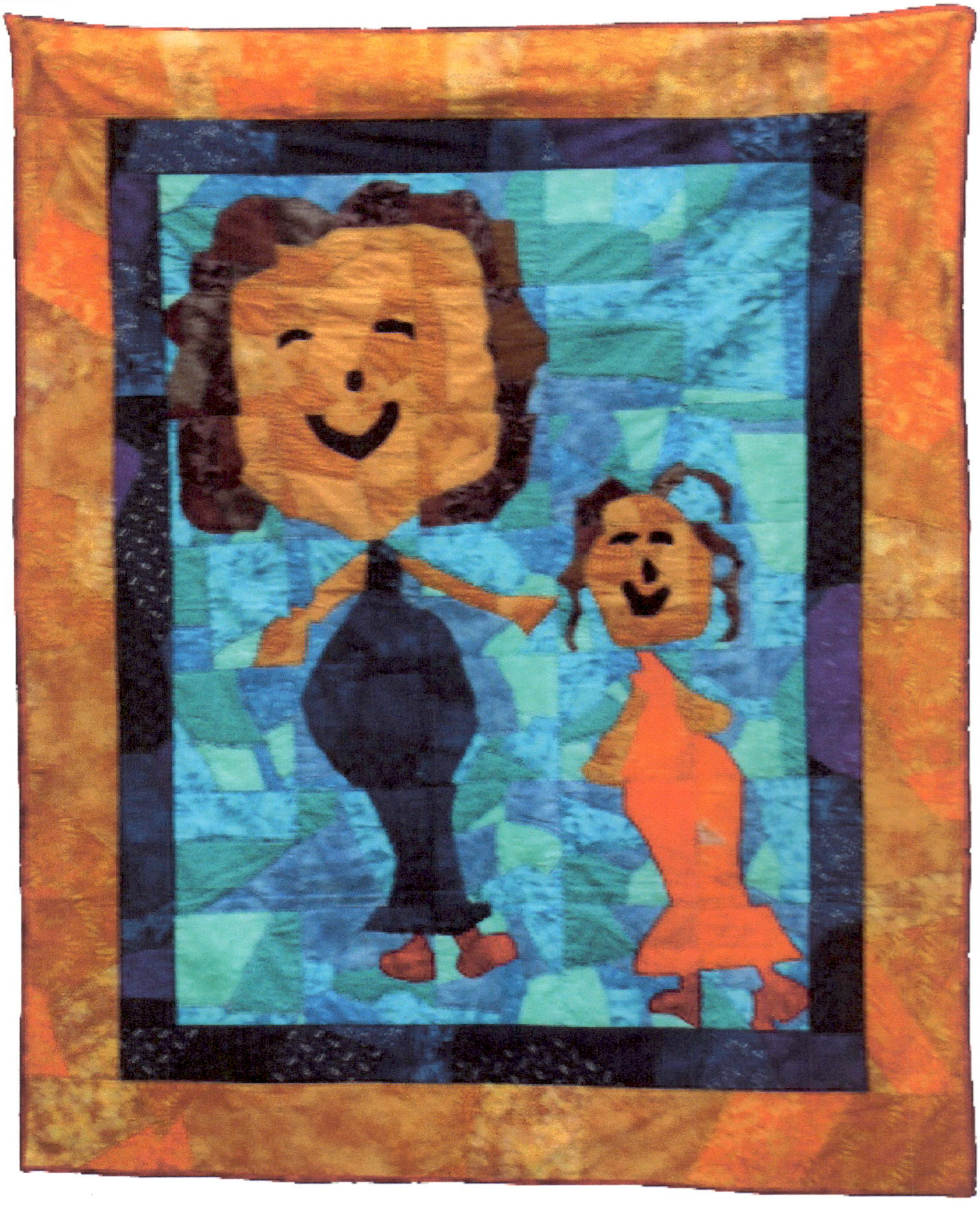

Chapter 7

Large Size Quilts - Technique 2

In this chapter, I will teach you how to take a picture like this, and turn it into a large bed quilt.

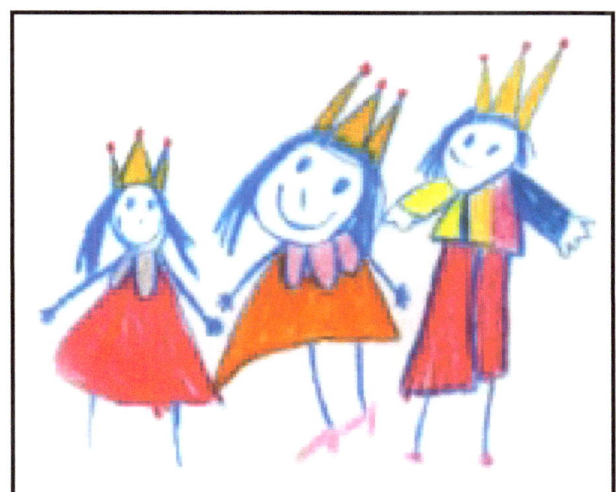

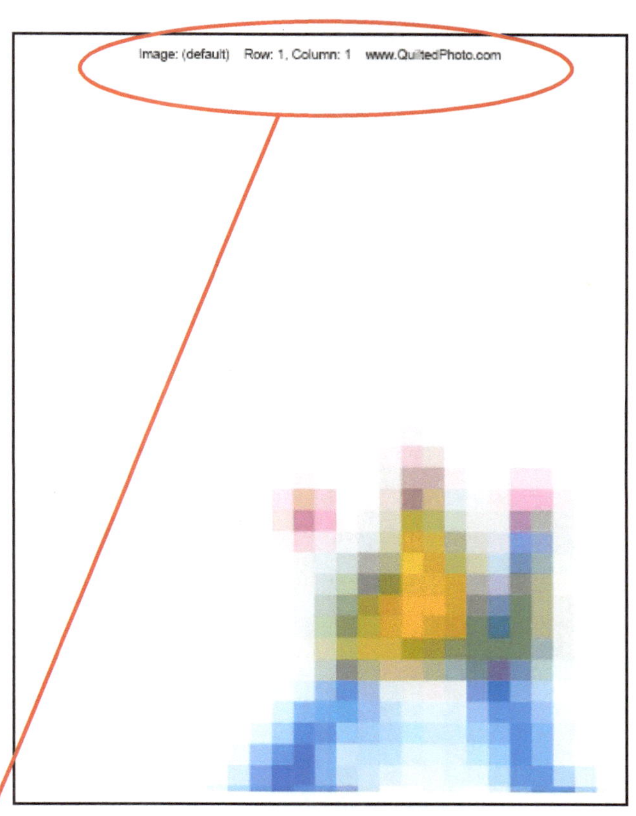

For this technique, I'm going to present some ideas that are different than any I've ever presented before, I'm also going to give you some quilting suggestions and a few ideas on how to finish your quilt.

The pattern for this technique has several pages and each page is labeled with rows and columns. Rows go across and columns go up and down.

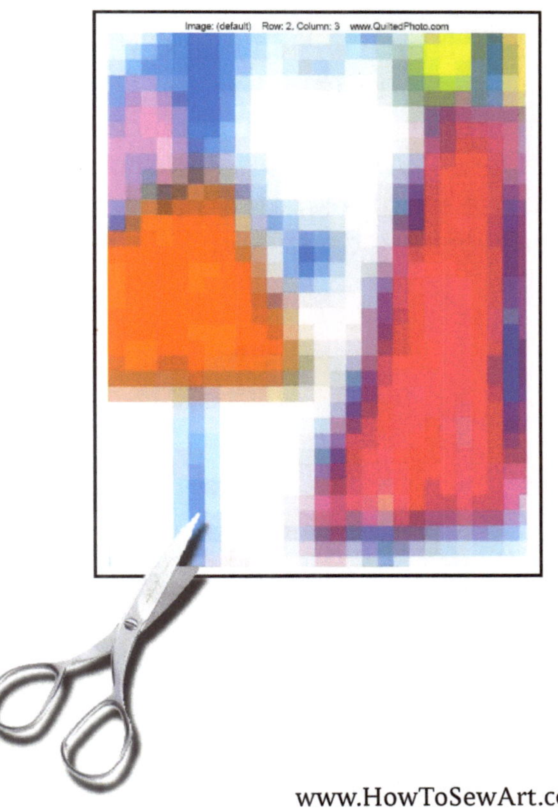

To prepare your pattern, cut the white borders off of the left side and off the bottom of the paper. Removing the 1/4" borders make it easy to tape the pages together, first in columns and then in rows. Use tape to form the columns. Then pin the columns together to create the whole pattern (diagram on next page).

For this technique, I don't want you to tape the columns together because we're going to use these columns and this paper pattern differently than the previous technique.

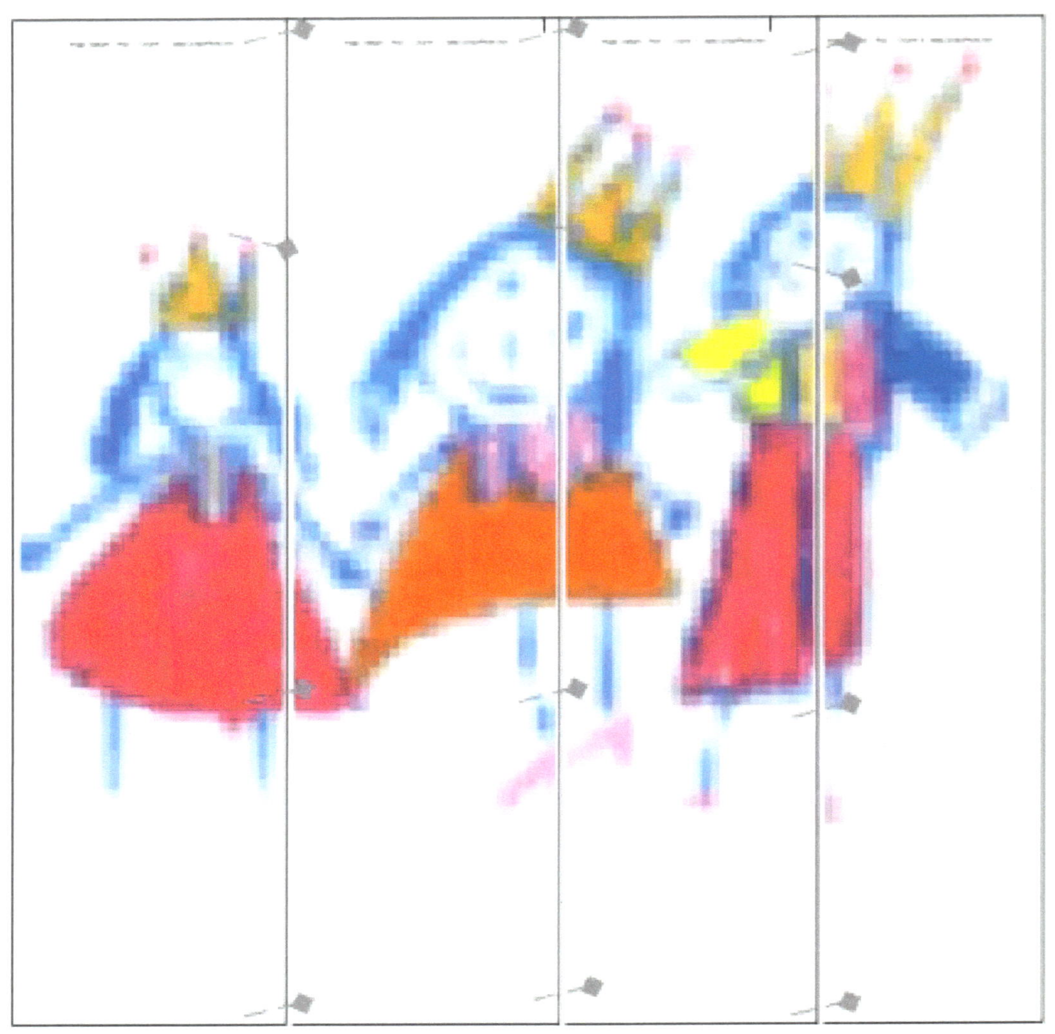

Pin the columns together.

The next step is to section off the pattern pieces of the picture with a marker or pen. Draw a border around the pieces. Take the marker and section off the pieces, following the colors. The diagram on the right is a close up of a small area. Note that you will be working on the whole pattern at this stage.

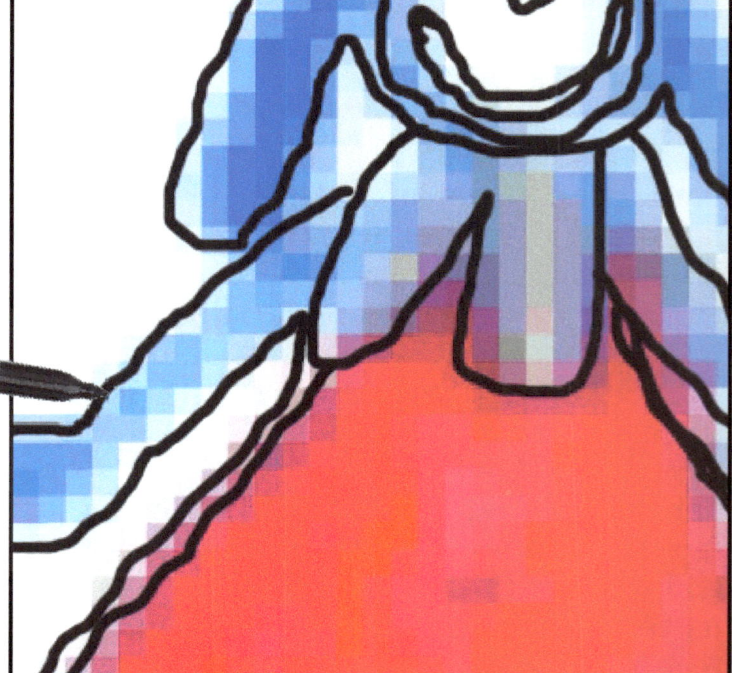

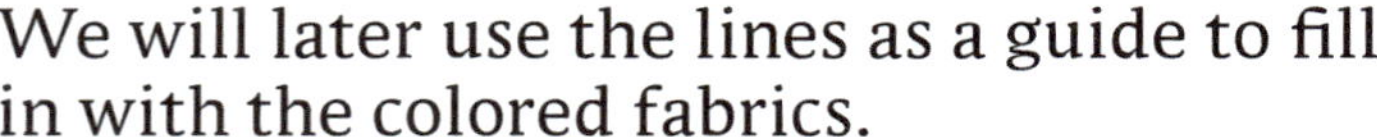

We will later use the lines as a guide to fill in with the colored fabrics.

Now, remove the pins to take the columns apart. Measure the width of your column. Measure down the length of your column the same measurement as the width to mark and cut the column into square blocks. (approximately 8" x 8").

The reason I have instructed you to cut the pattern into blocks is because it will be much easier to make a large quilt if you are working with smaller sections such as 8" square blocks.

So you're going to cut out and iron down the fabric pieces according to the colors on the pattern. As you can see, I have some possible fabric sections below.

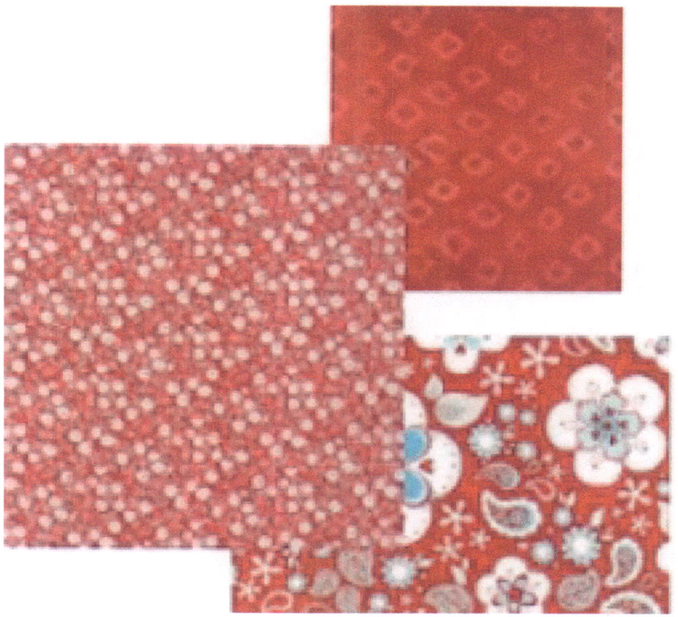

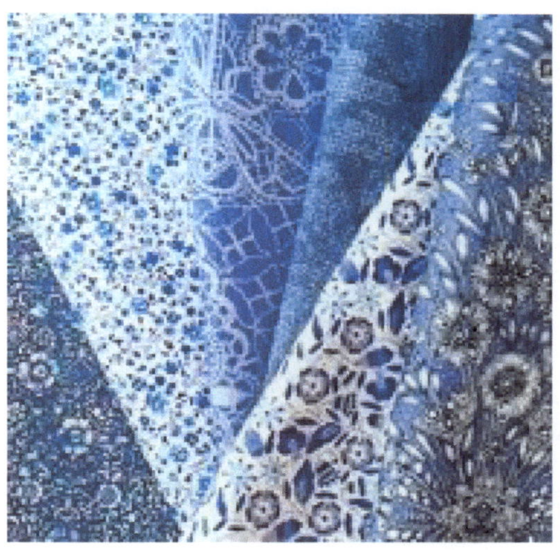

Now, to begin putting the quilt squares together, you will place the pattern block on the table. You must extend the fabric pieces a little more than 1/2" past the edge of the pattern block. The purpose of the extra fabric is to leave enough for needed seam allowance. Place Fusible Tricot on top of the pattern with the adhesive (rough) side facing upward.

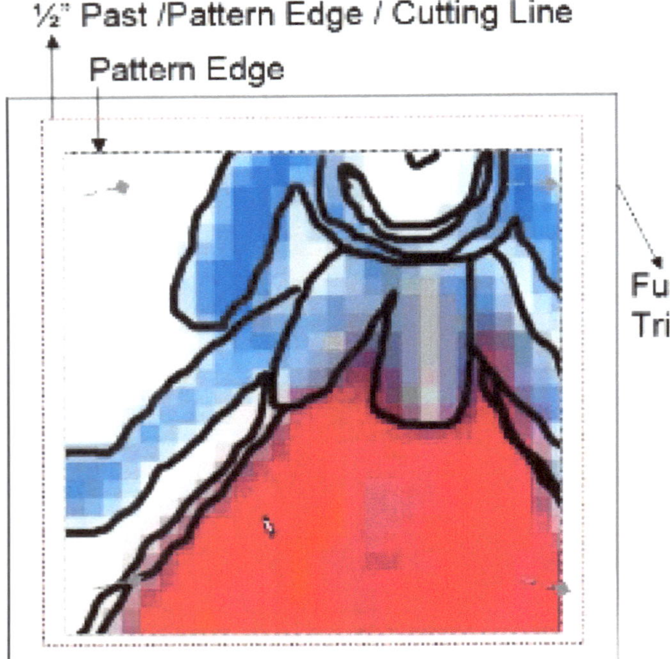

Before you start adding fabric, pin the tricot to the pattern from the back side. If you pin from the back side, it will be easy to remove the pins without disturbing the fabric later.

The reason I suggest Fusible Tricot for this technique is because it will remain very soft after applying fabric and quilting. Cut random fabric pieces to fill in the pattern according to color. I suggest using several different fabrics of the same color to cover the block. Keep in mind that you're going to have to stitch every raw cut edge in some sort of way, so do not make the pieces unnecessarily small. Remember to extend fabric pieces 1/2" or more past the block edge.

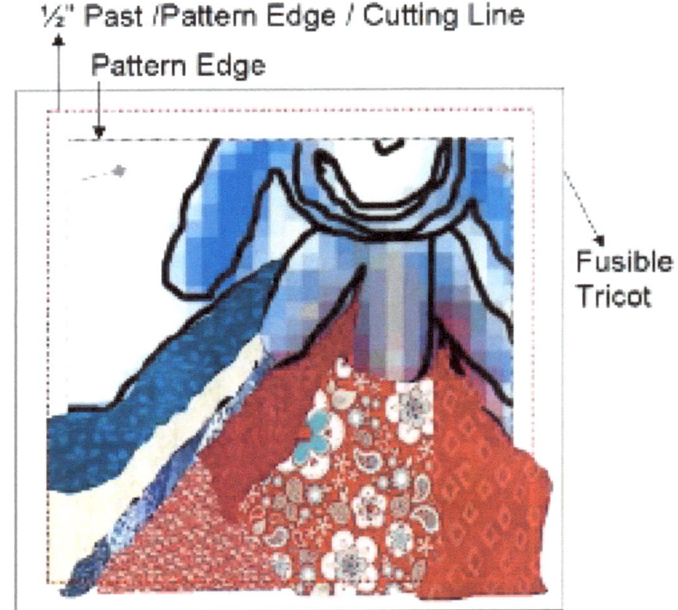

After you position a few pieces of fabric (or after each piece), iron the fabric pieces onto the fusible tricot, taking care not to touch the iron on the areas of the tricot that are not covered by fabric. The fusible tricot has a glue that will melt onto your iron if heat is applied directly.

There are also small craft irons that can be used for this process. Continue until you fill up the whole pattern block with the appropriate fabrics.

On the next page, you'll see what a block will look like when it's all filled in with fabrics. It is starting to look very different than just the drawing. It is very exciting!

Now I have to tell you a story. I've made a

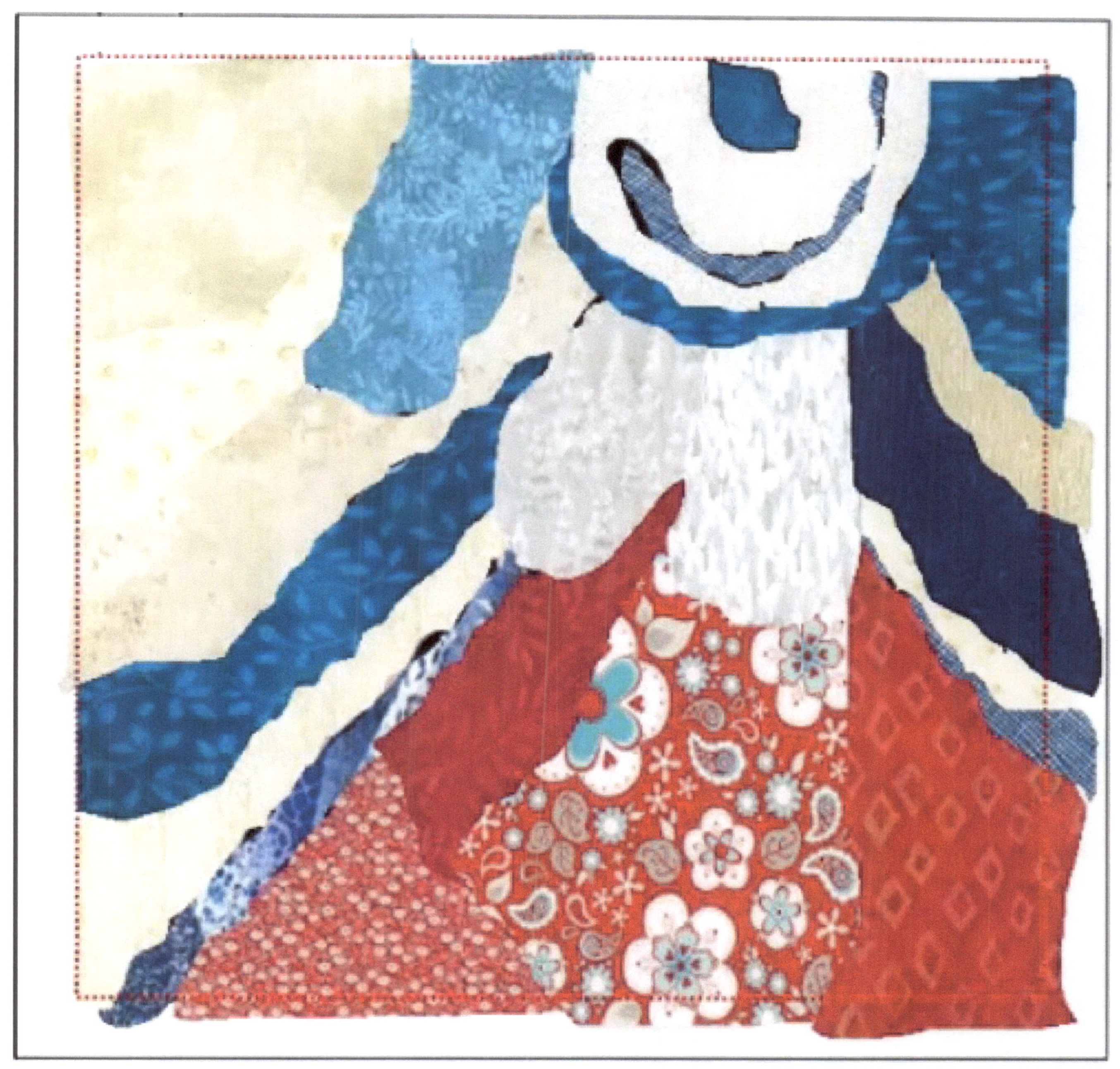

lot of quilts and most of them are pretty spectacular. Some of them were even award winning! However, when my daughter was 7 years old, I made a quilt from one of her drawings just as I am instructing in this chapter. See the quilt on page 60.

I was working on her quilt and when she came home from school and saw it spread out on the floor, she gasped and couldn't hide her excitement! She has never shown this kind of excitement for any of my other "award winning" quilts! She couldn't care less about my quilts.... but she cared about "her quilt"!

When you look at a child's drawing on a small piece of paper, it's really cute, but the impact is spectacular when it's transformed into a giant quilt. I hope you will try this technique and make a big quilt because it's really great. Children really love them!

So, now we're going to add the stitching. To do that, you must first remove the paper

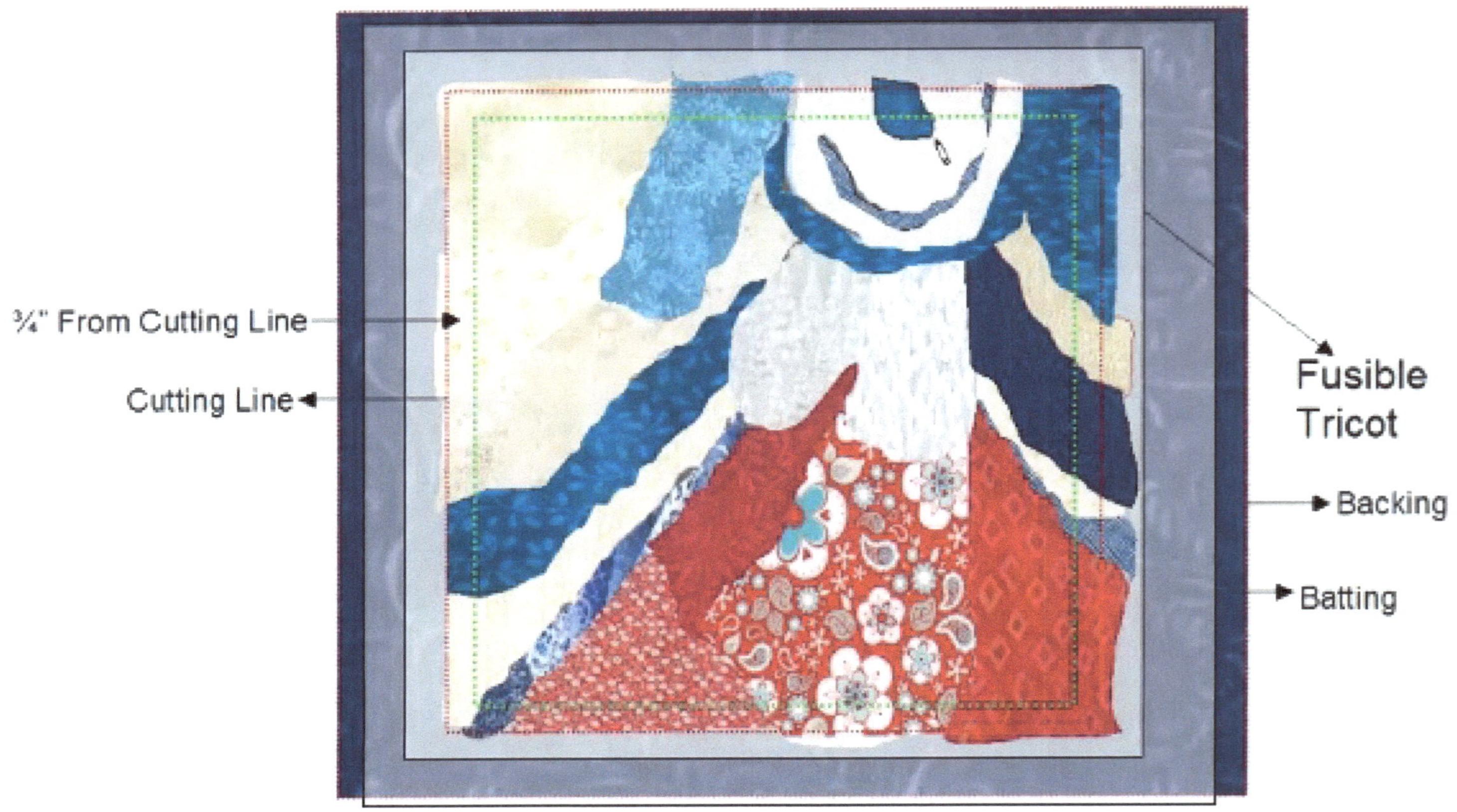

pattern by unpinning and removing the paper pattern off the back of the block. Place batting and backing behind the quilt block. Then you can begin your stitching.

When you add your quilting, stay 3/4" inside of where the pattern edge is located. Don't do any stitching past that line.

Thread
I like to use variegated threads. I change the thread based on the colors in the picture.

Since we have several red colors for the dress on the block above, I might pick red variegated thread to do all the red stitching. Likewise with the background, I'll use beige there and blue on the arm and everywhere else there is blue.

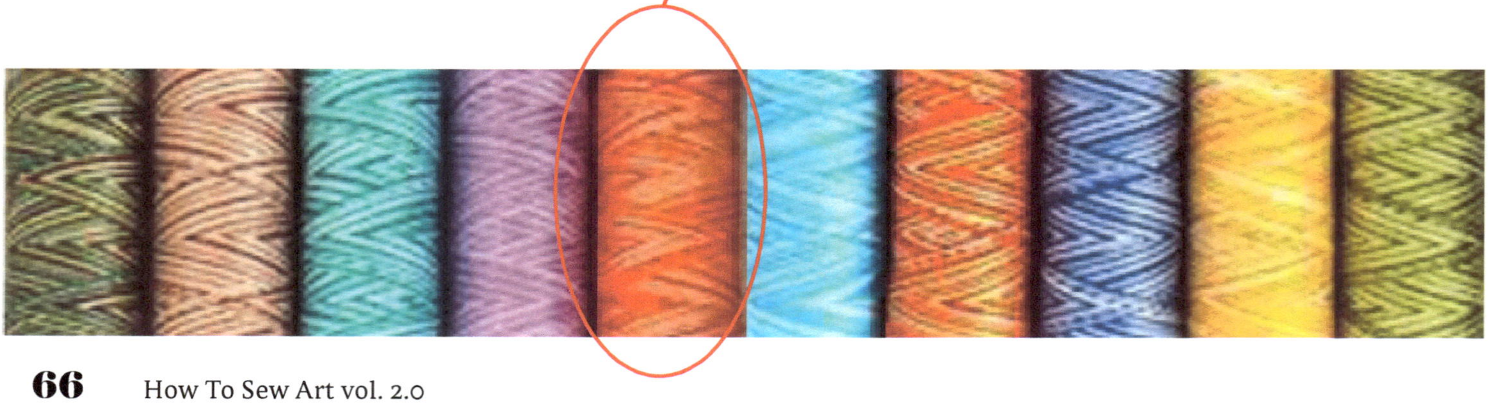

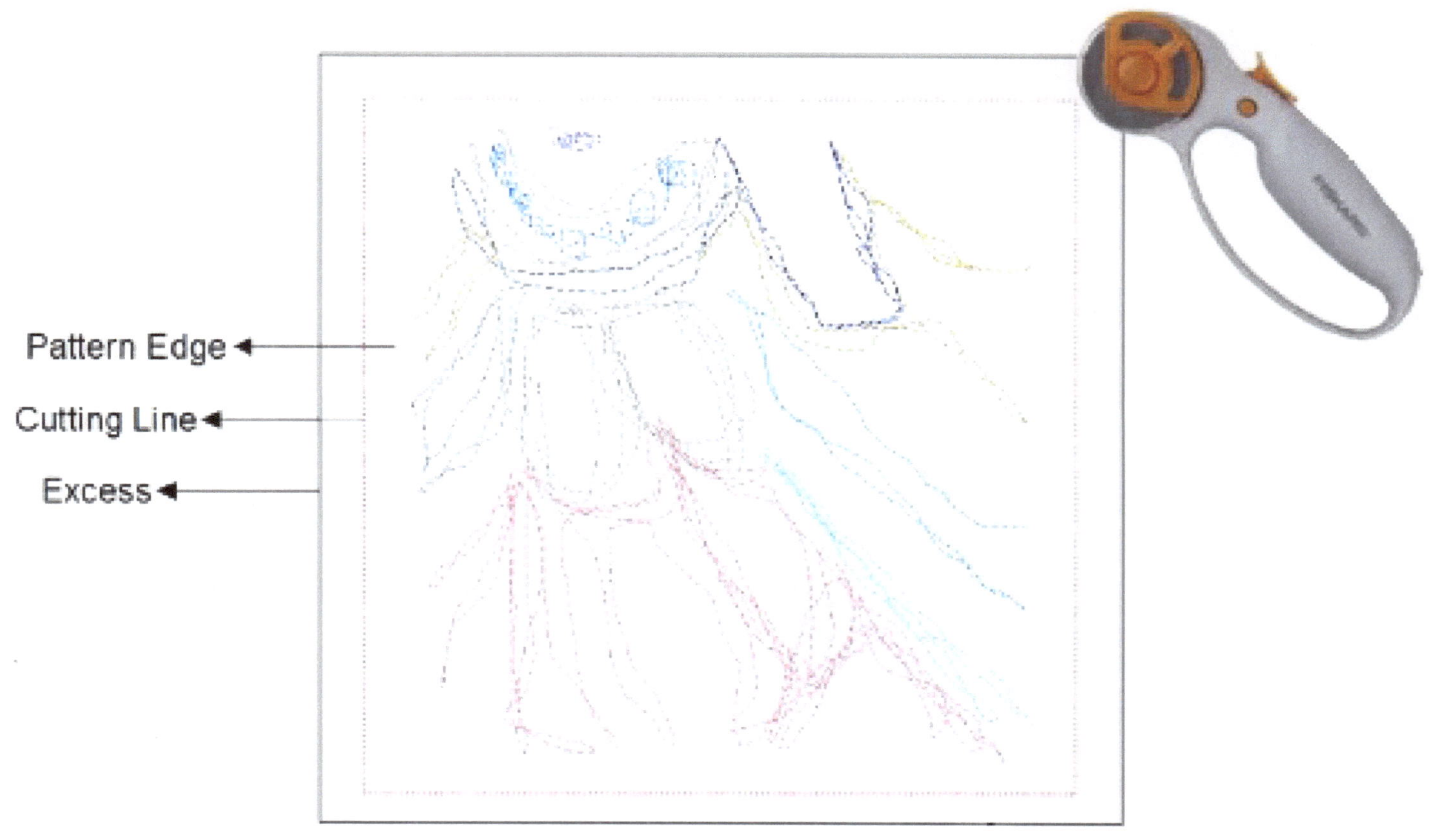

Stitching
Stitch each area of the block (according to color), filling the areas with stitching as much or as little as you like. For this example, I used straight stitching, but I used all of the fancy stitches on my sewing machine (changing to a different stich for each edge) for my daughters quilt on page 60. I have more ideas for quilting in chapter 9.

After you get done with the whole block, turn it over to the back side and cut away the excess tricot, batting and backing. Remember, to cut away the excess on the cutting line which is 1/2" away from the pattern edge. Use your rotary cutter and ruler and cut all of the four sides. You will end up with your stitched block and half-inch seam allowance all around. The cut block should be 8 1/2" x 8 1/2".

This is what a finished block should look like.

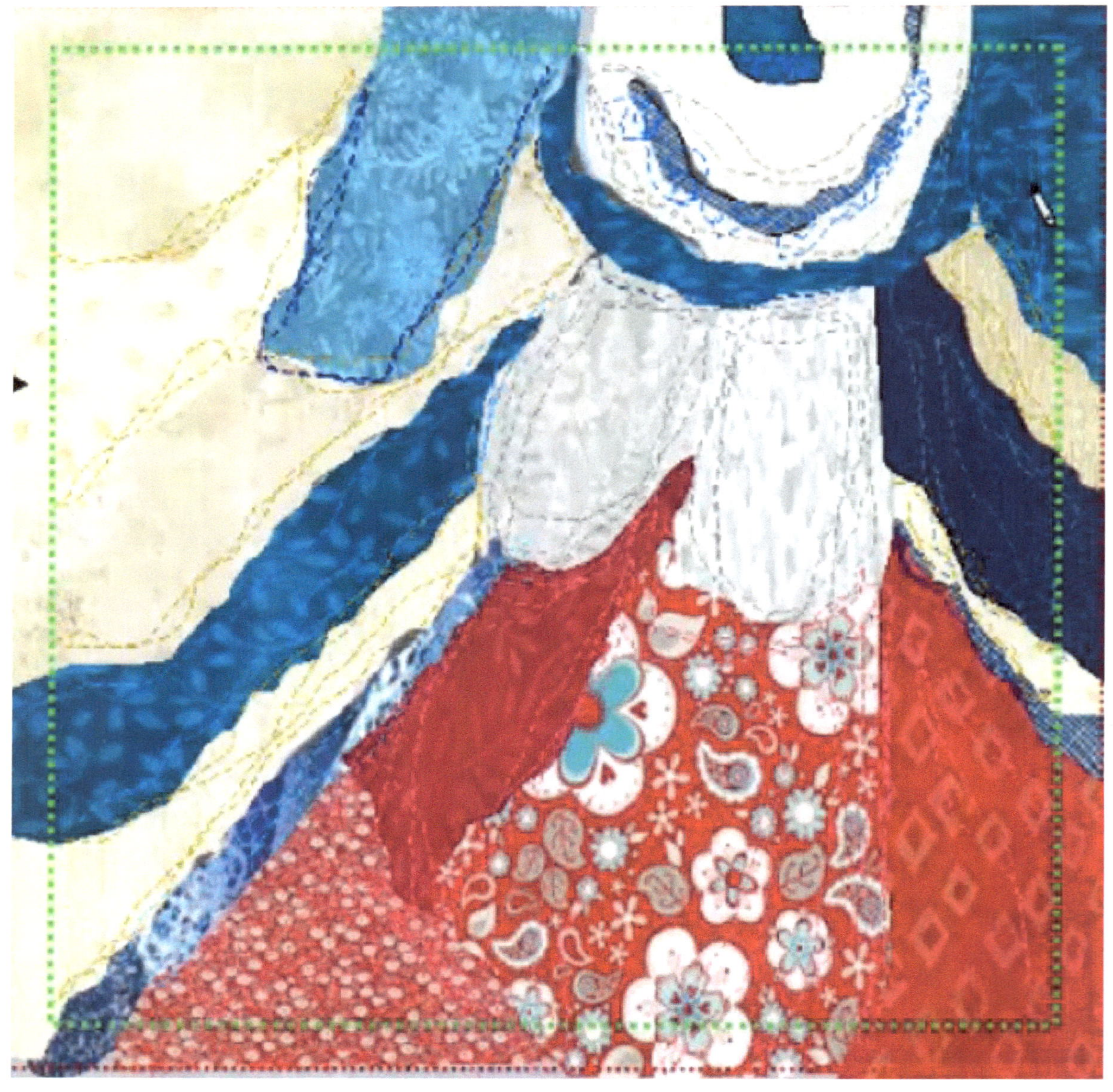

Chapter 8

Quilt As You Go - Technique 2

Now I want to show you how to put the quilt blocks together with a quilt-as-you-go technique. Before I explain that to you, if you're comfortable sewing a big quilt, you can absolutely sew your blocks together and quilt in the traditional way.

I've added this "Quilt-As-You-Go" technique because it's easier for those who are not comfortable stitching large quilts. It can be challenging ... I know it was challenging for me. You can quilt one block at a time instead of being taunted with the idea of feeding such a large quilt through your sewing machine.

After you have all of your stitched blocks, turn them face to face keeping the blocks in the proper order. In the diagram below, we're looking at two blocks with the fronts facing each other. The back of the block is facing towards us.

Fold back the batting and the backing away from the fronts and stitch a scant (just short of a 1/2" seam) only stitching the block fronts together.

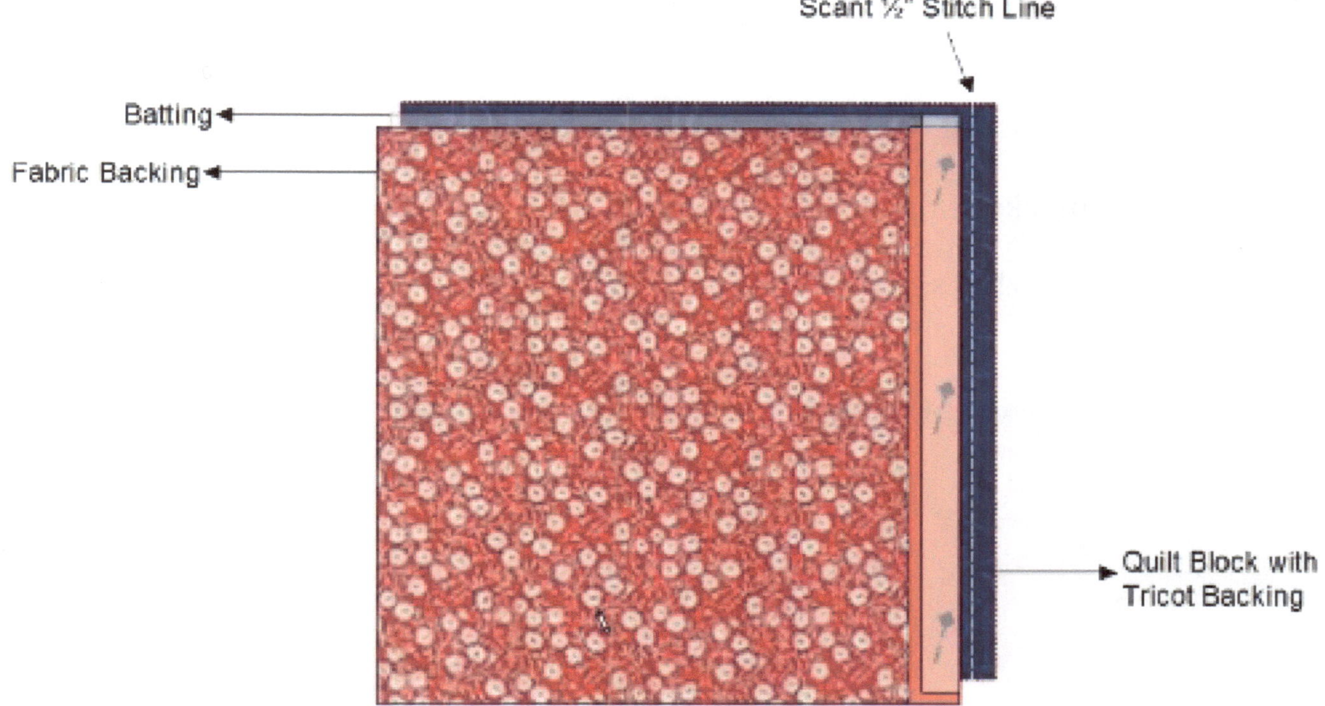

Place two squares (or columns) right sides together. Fold & pin the backing and batting away from the Quilt Block. Stitch the Quilt Blocks together with a scant ½" seam. Cut away ¼" of the seam allowance.

Use a few pins to keep the batting and backing folded away from the stitched seam. Now cut away 1/4" of the seam allowance.

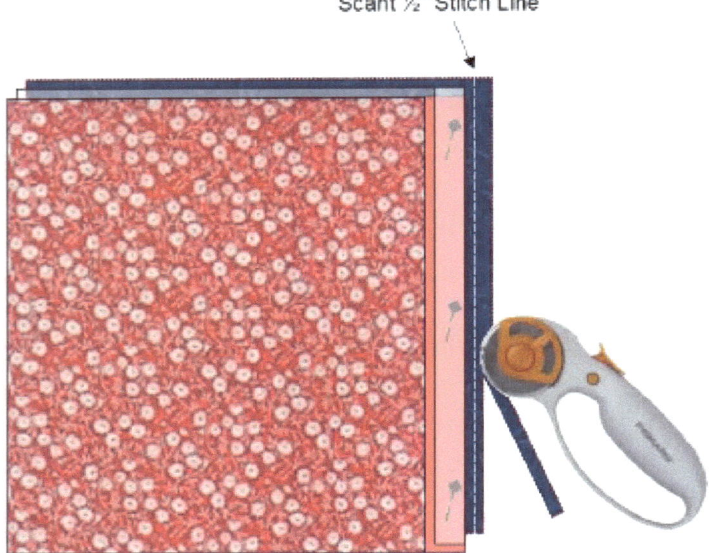

Cut away ¼" of the seam allowance.

Open up those two blocks and place the fronts down towards the table. The next step is to carefully iron that seam open so that it opens flat.

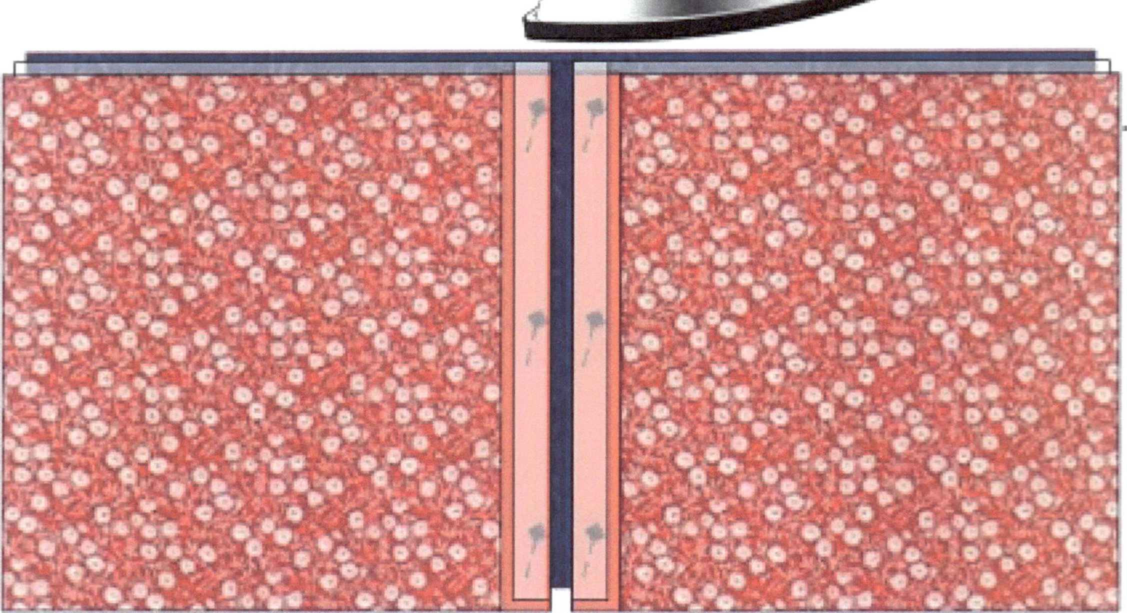

Press the seam allowance open with and iron.

After ironing the seam, release the batting and keep the backing pinned out of the way. Use scissors to cut only the batting so that edges meet in the center. The goal is for the batting to lay down flat without any overlap.

Do not cut all the way through to the front. Only cut the batting so that the edges of the batting meet in the center. It will be like one continuous piece of batting.

Put all of the squares in each row together the same exact way to create the rows.

Optional: If your quilting does not meet at the center of the seam, now is the time to carefully add a line of straight stitching.

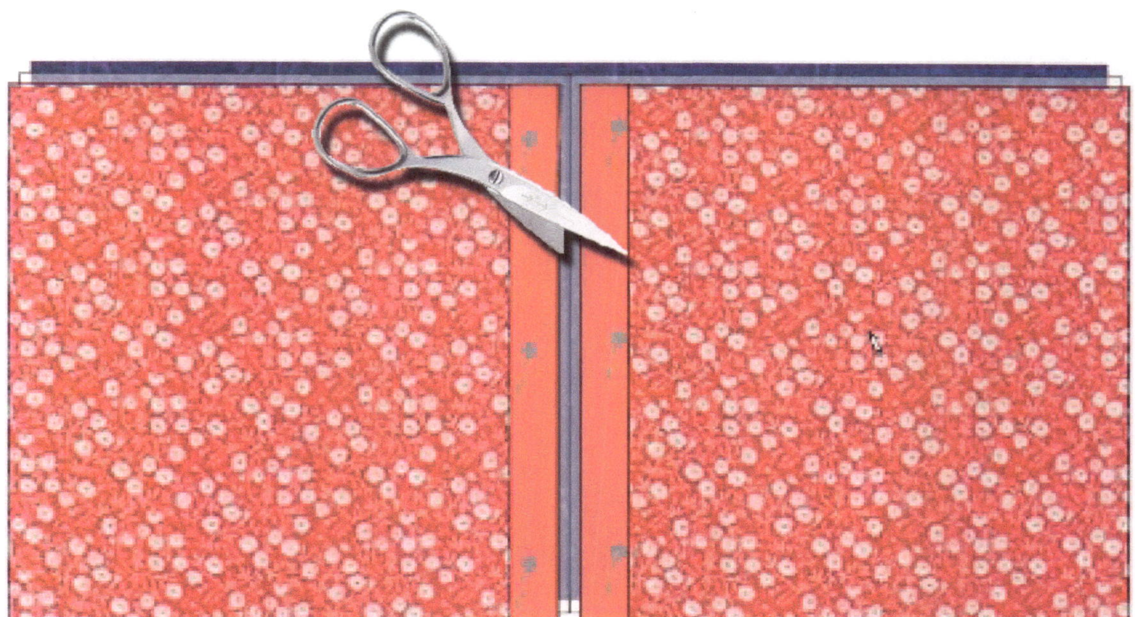

Release the batting keeping the backing fabric pinned out of the way. Use scissors to cut the edges of the batting to meet in the center. This will keep the seam flat.

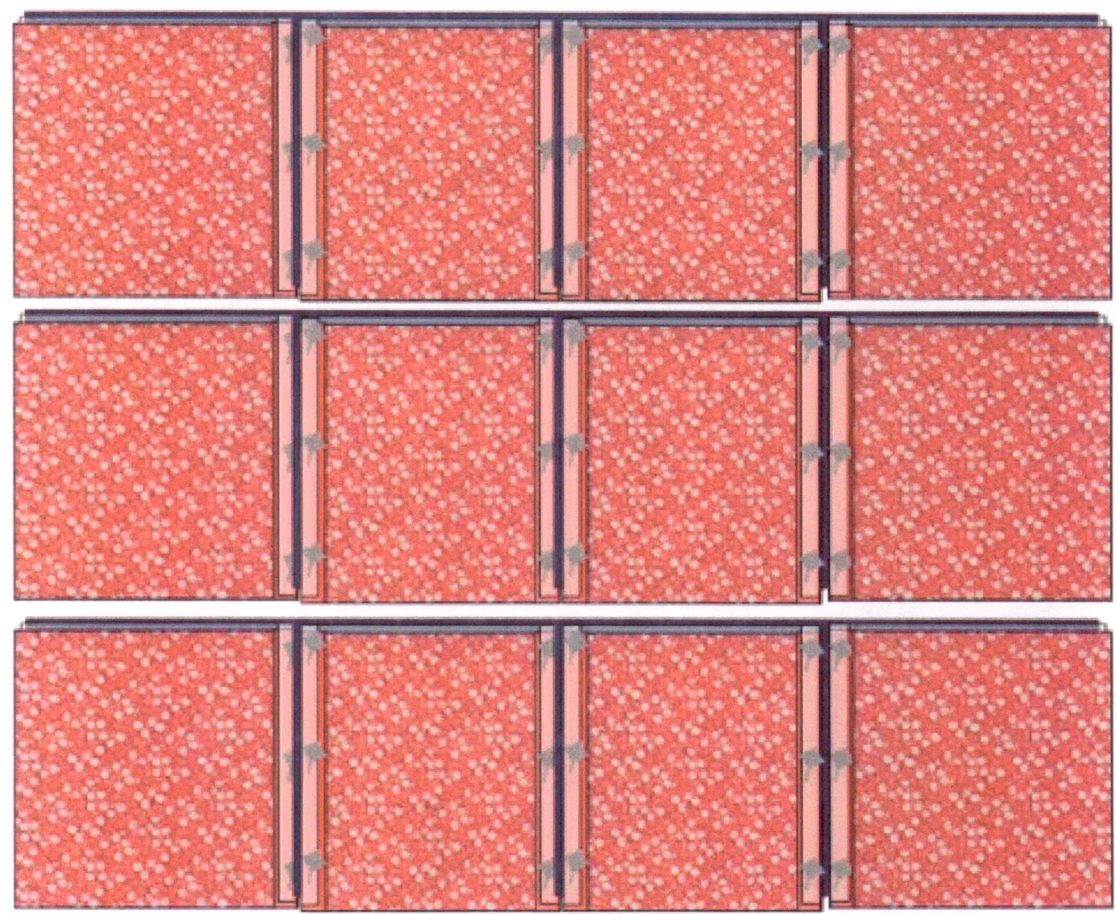

After you put all of your rows together, remove the pins from one side of the backing. (This is a close up of two blocks, but you will be working on a row).

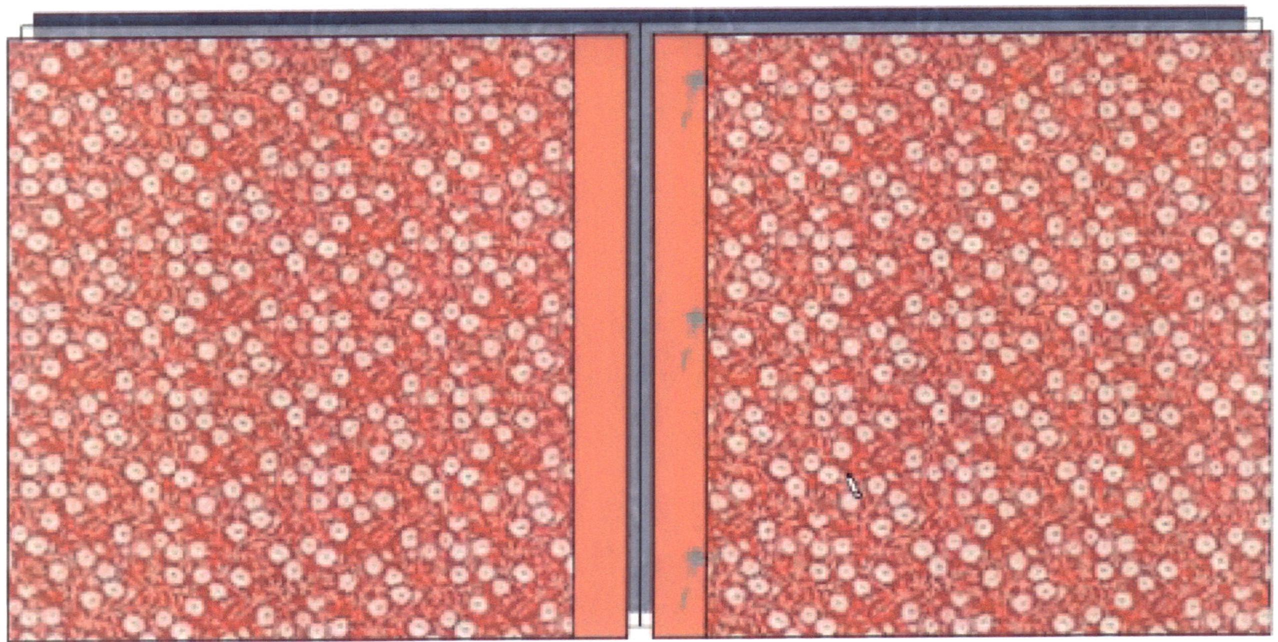

Remove the pins from one side.

Fold the unpinned side over, towards the center. Trim away the excess so that it lays down flat.

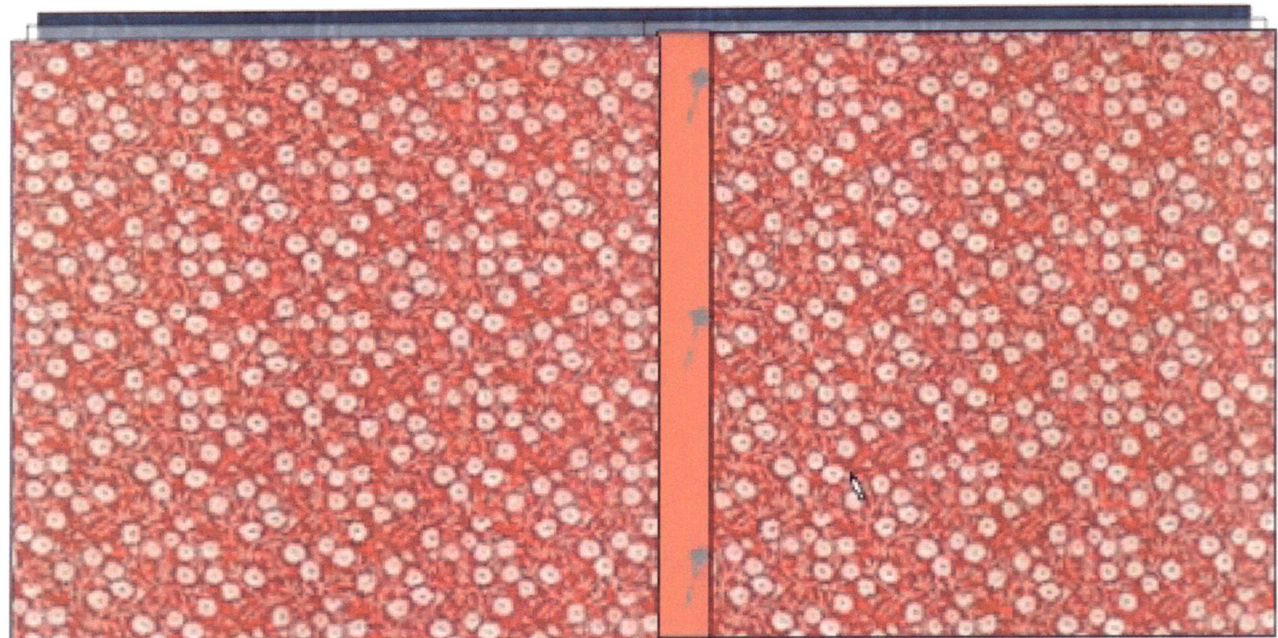

Unfold one side of the backing. Trim away excess fabric to make it lay flat.

You can now remove the pins from the opposite side. Fold under the the raw edge 1/4".

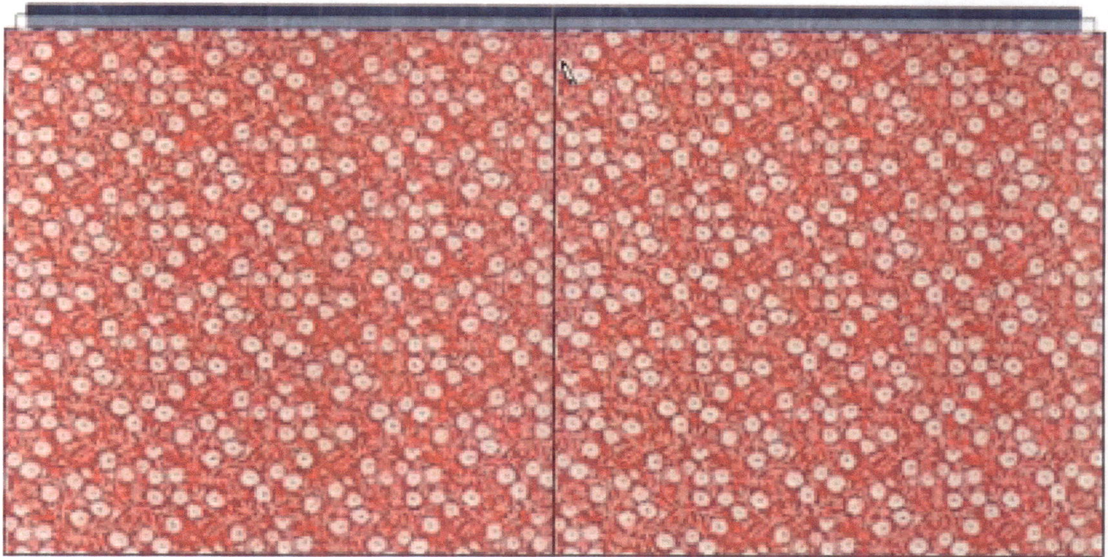

Finally, to finish the row, whip stitch or hand stitch the backing seam so that the seam is closed and finished.

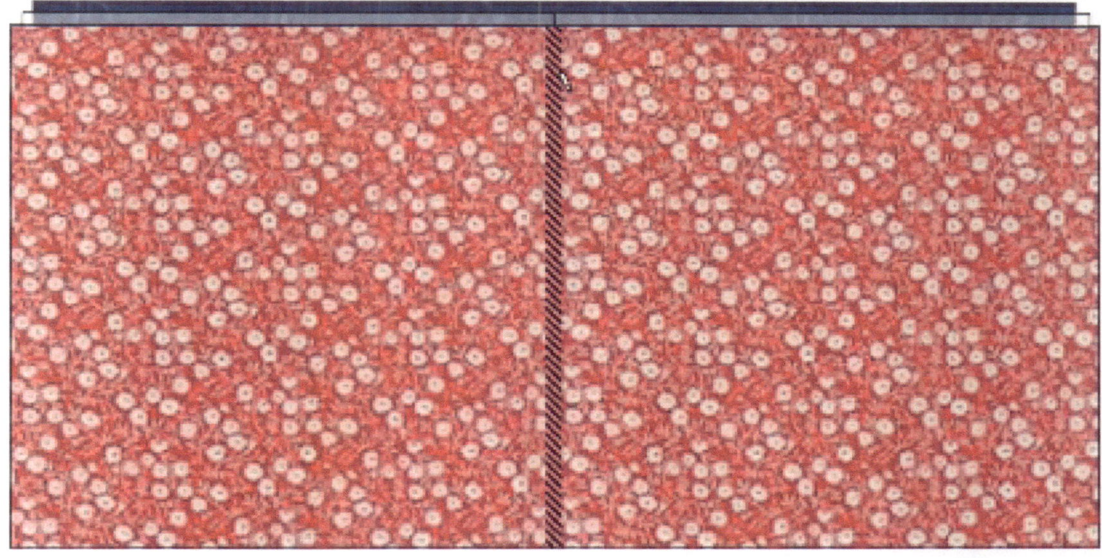

After you finish making the rows, sew the larger sections you just created using the same process.

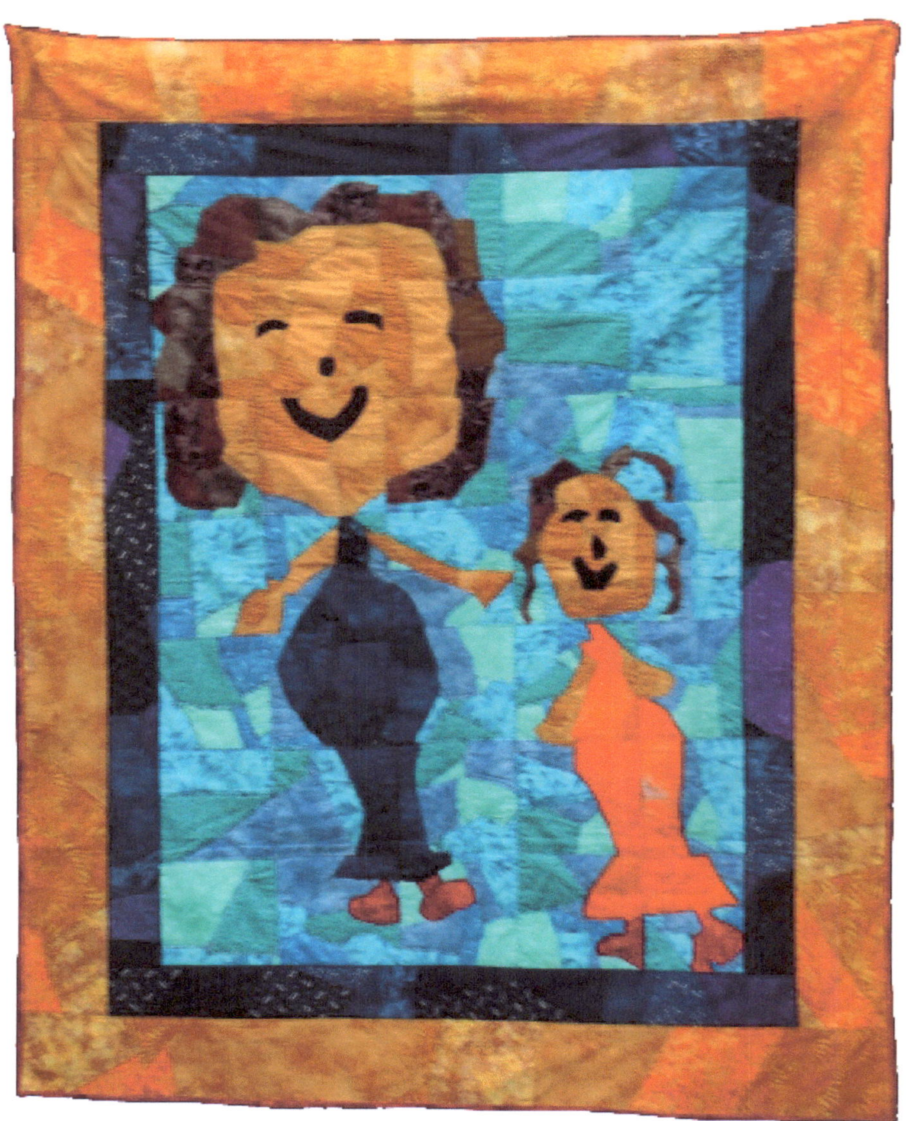

Close Up View Of Stitching

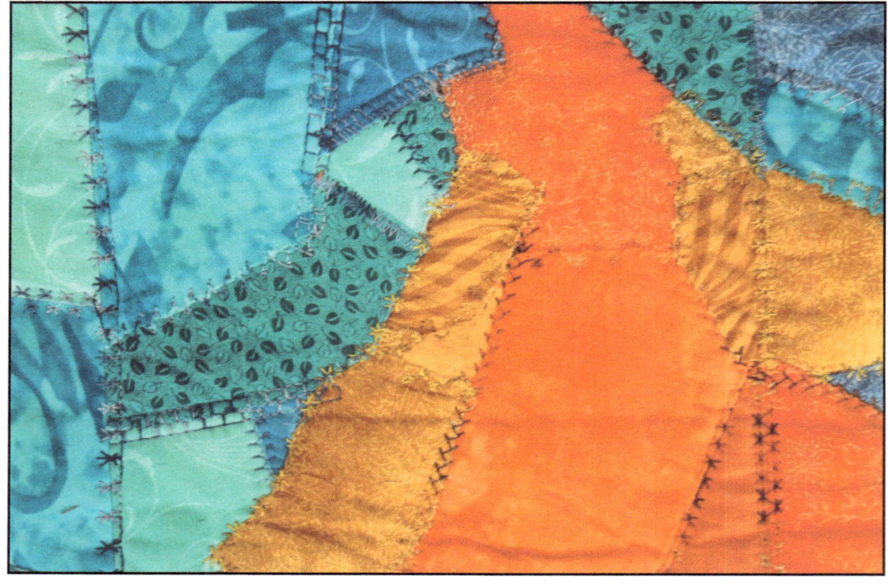

Chapter 9

Doodlemotion And More!

Most of the time, I do use straight stitching for quilting, but there are some other stitching ideas that I call "Doodlemotion" that are very exciting.

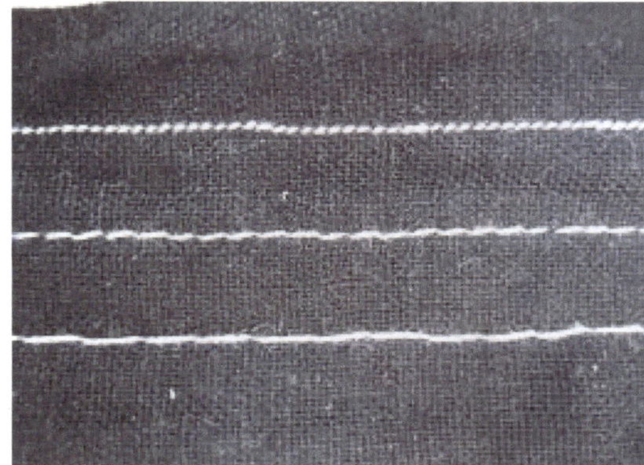

If you're going to use a straight stitch, one of the options you can use is a meandering straight stitch, which a lot of people like and it's very good. If that's what you like, then that's perfect.

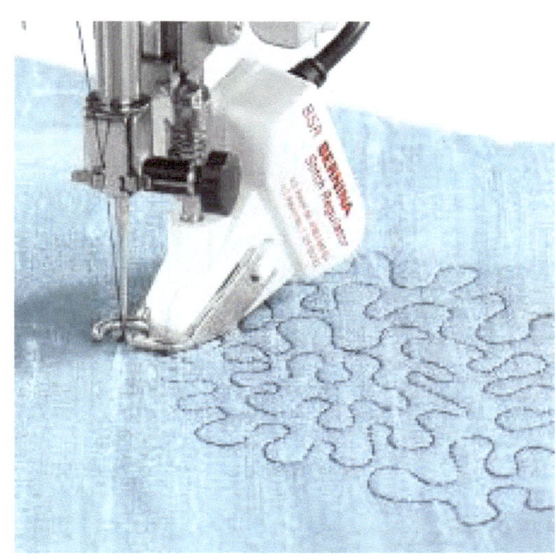

Here is a close-up of some of my quilts. You can see that I used straight stitching, following the shapes of the pieces. That's been my style for a long time and I call it "Doodlemotion" because it feels like I'm

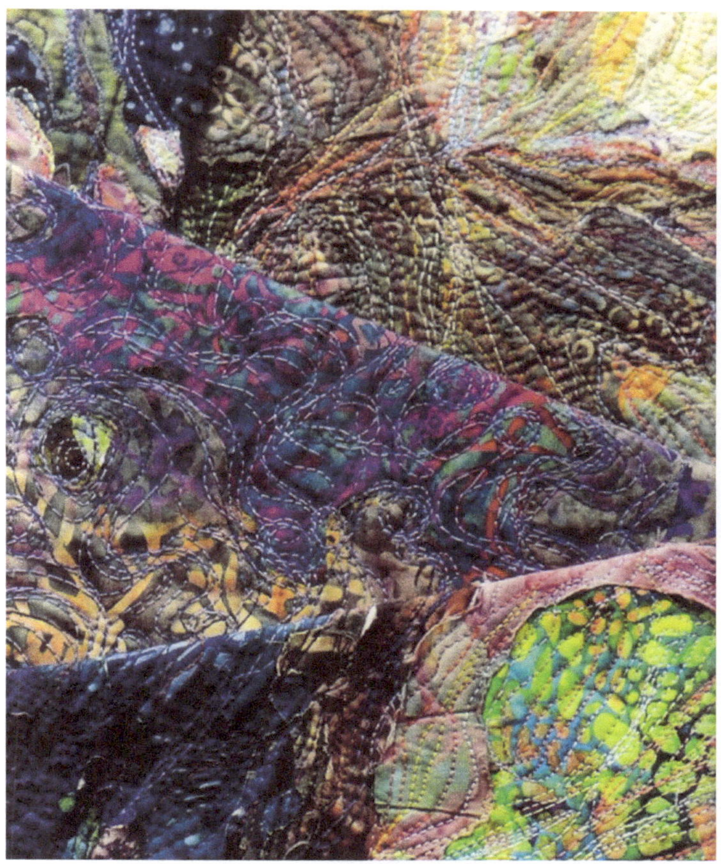

doodling with my sewing machine. My style is to use a lot of stitching, but you should be aware that more stitching will cause the quilt to be stiff and less stitching will make a softer quilt. For large sized or bed quilts, I would choose to do less stitching.

The most obvious way to stitch the quilts you've learned in this book is with straight stitching following the same direction as the crayon/brush strokes on the original picture. You simply mimic the contours that are drawn by the artist. You don't have to guess how to stitch it.

Another idea for stitching that I think is particularly good, and I used it on the quilt that I made for my daughter (page 74), is using all of the fancy stitches my sewing machine has. On every seam, I switched the fancy stitch and stitched down the edges. Each of the seams has a different fancy stitch. I used all of stitches that I never use and I probably haven't used them since. The children's quilts are whimsical and this way of quilting is also whimsical.

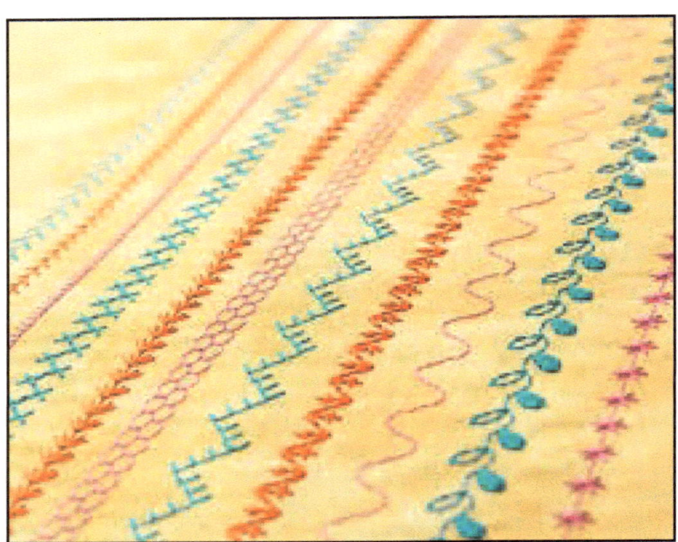

I only added the stitches on the edges of the random fabric pieces, so this quilt remained very soft. Another idea is to use just a simple zigzag stitch.

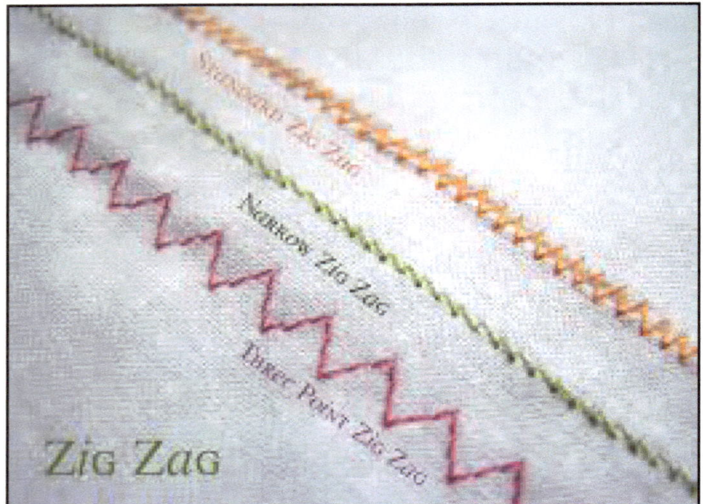

You can use the zig zag stitch on the seams, or you can also free motion using that zig zag stitch. I find that very exciting. This is another idea that I think is fabulous...using a combination of zigzag and "Doodlemotion"!

Here are some examples of using the zig zag stitch and "Doodlemotion" all mixed together. I think this is a fabulous idea and I hope it's opening your eyes to think about the quilting a little bit differently for this technique. I love this idea. It's very exciting!

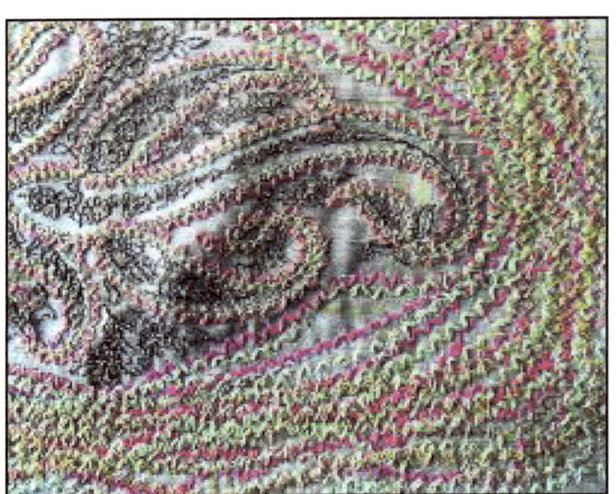

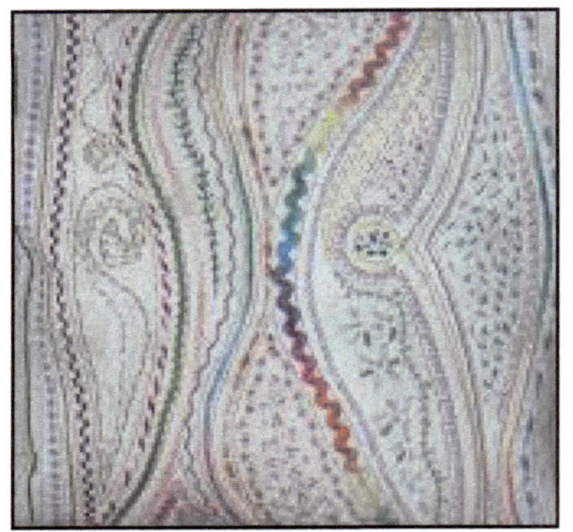

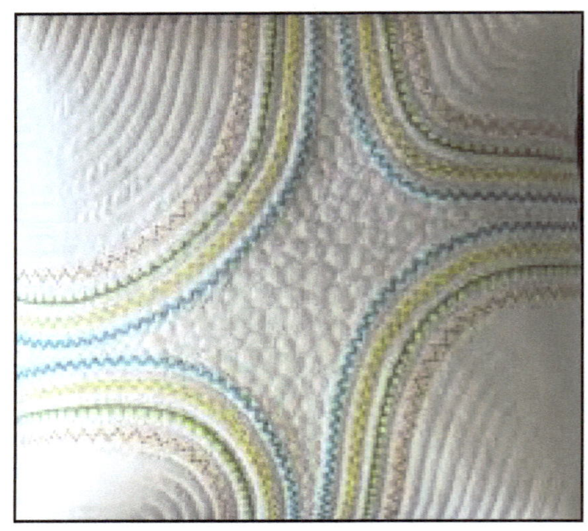

Chapter 10

Finishing

Now I want to talk about finishing. I will first give some border possibilities, and then I will move on to some basic finishing concepts. If you are a quilter, you probably already know how to do these basic bindings and finishes, but visual references are included if you need them.

Borders and bindings make a huge difference in how the final quilt looks. I want to show you several options.

1. You can add a little border.

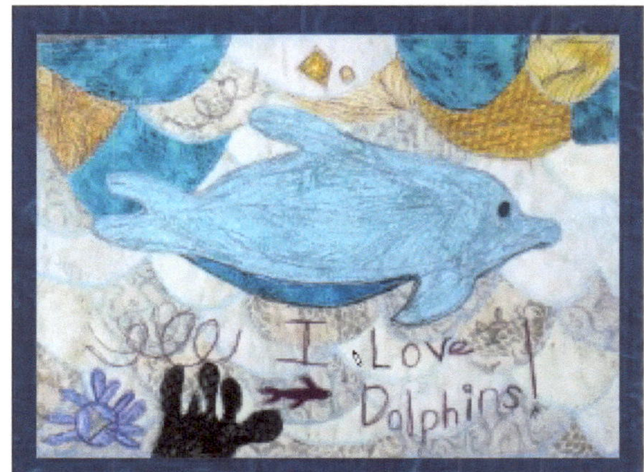

2. You can even add a second border. You can also use several fabrics to create the second border. I used all of the blue fabrics randomly to create the border in this example. I really like this option, so I wanted to show it to you.

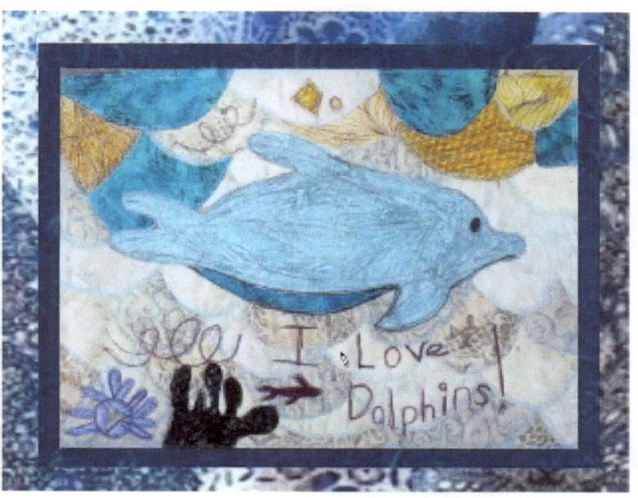

3. Of course you can add a small binding to finish it off.

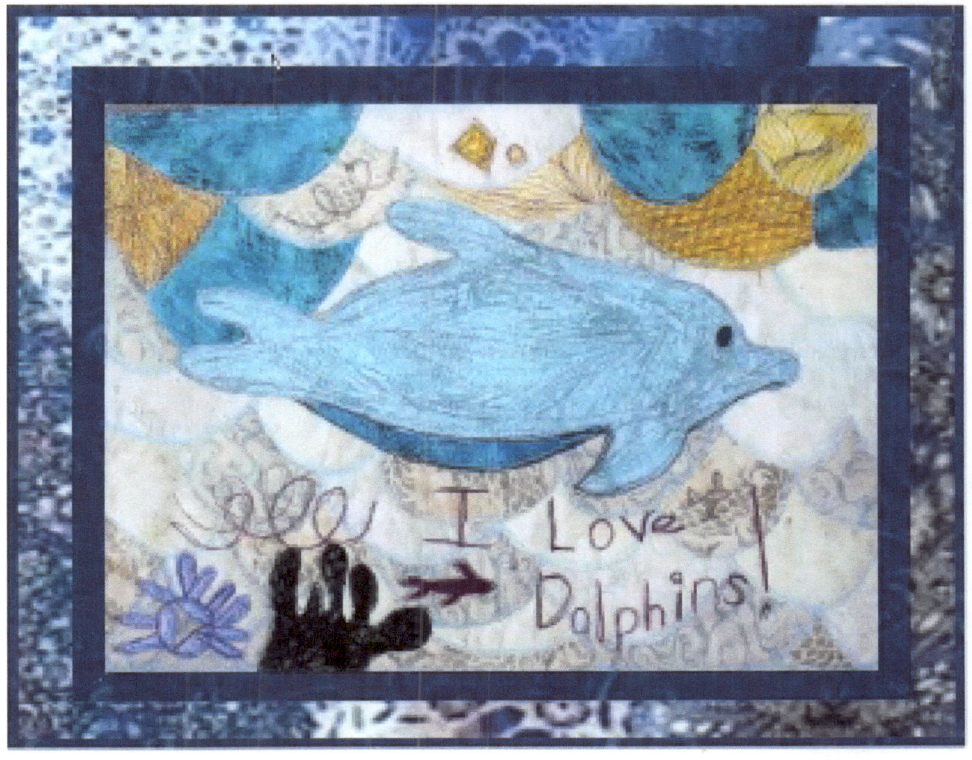

4. I also like doing a more modern type of finish by making it invisible and just having the stitched quilt only with no border. That's all up to you.

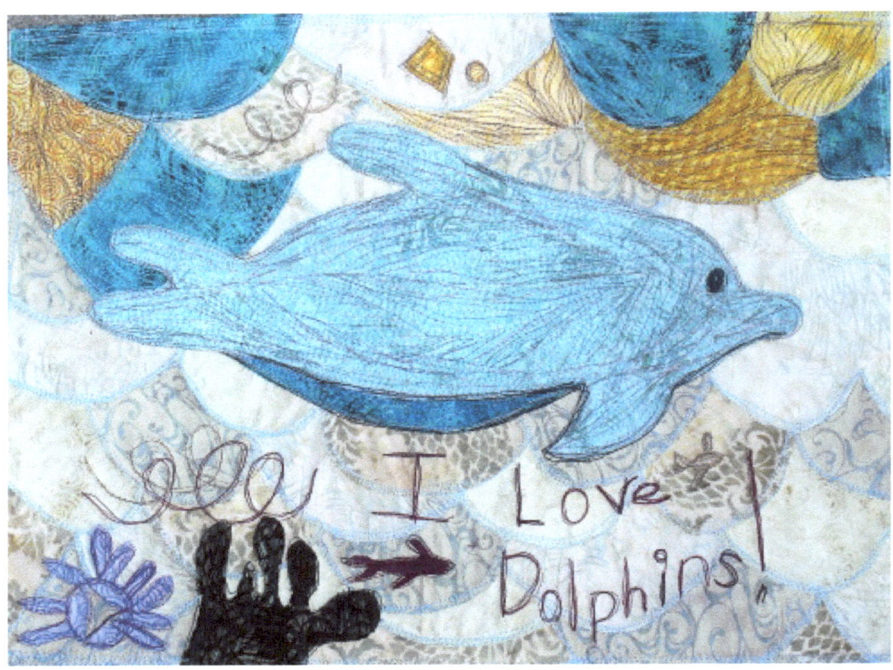

On To The Basics...

Even though you have made your amazing quilt top, the project is not complete until you have made it suitable for display. There are many ways you can finish your quilt top. I will discuss each of the available options in this chapter. The options range from borders, to bindings, to stretching your quilt top like a canvas!

Trimming The Quilt

Even if you have fused your pieces perfectly following the pattern, your quilt may not have perfectly straight edges with squared corners after you add the quilting. The stitching may distort the shape slightly. However, it is okay if your quilt is not perfect. You can trim the edges.

If you want to add a border, trim the edges with your rotary cutter first. Trimming will make sure that your quilt hangs straight when displayed on a wall.

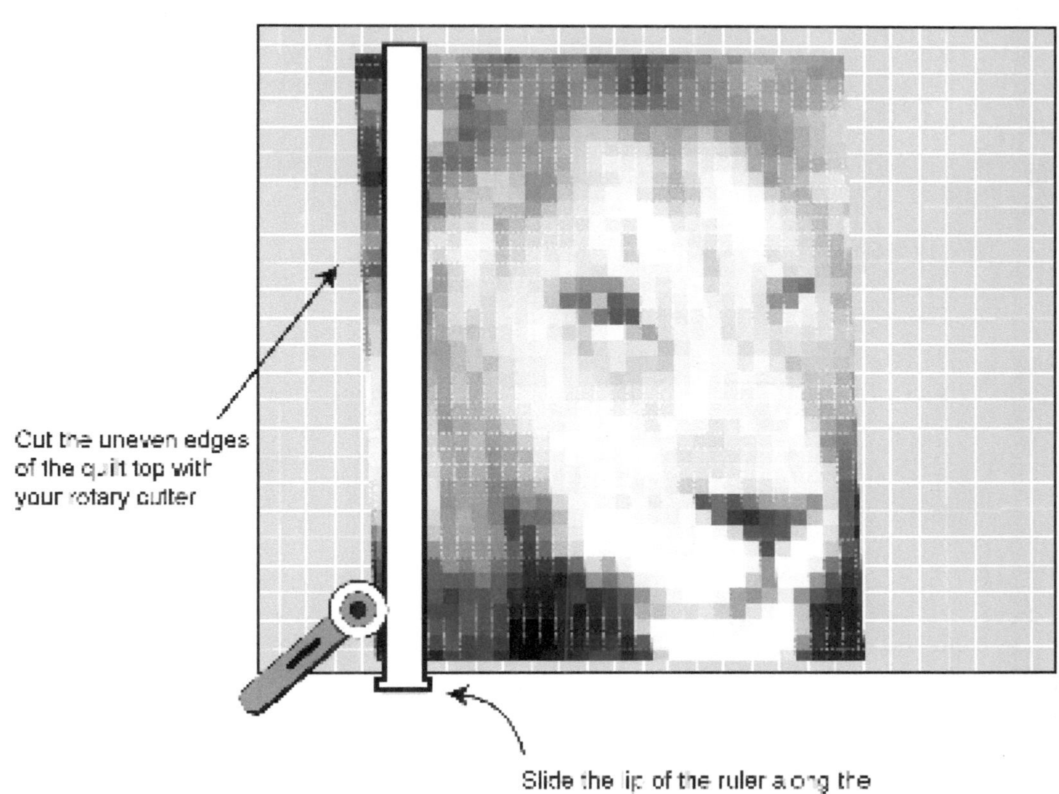

Adding Borders

A border is a straight strip of fabric sewn around the edges of your quilt to finish it.

A border can make your quilt even more beautiful but borders also have a practical purpose. Adding a border will make the edges of the quilt perfectly straight, and the corners will be perfectly squared. The border will make the quilted photo hang perfectly straight on the wall without any wavy edges. Another added bonus is that the border will increase the size of the quilt and provide another place to put decorative stitching.

Adding a border is a decision you will make after you see the finished quilt top. You can add one or two borders or have no border at all.

When you think about adding borders to your quilted photos, you can pretend you are adding a matting and frame. Pay attention to the way paper photographs are framed. Also look at how paintings and other works of art are finished. Notice how the colors relate to the artwork, and pay close attention to the proportion of the border in relation to the artwork. There are two types of borders - straight cut borders and mitered borders. I will explain both types.

To add a straight border, the first step is to measure at the center of the quilt in both directions. Be sure to measure in the center of the quilt because the edges of the quilt are probably stretched and are not accurate

Diagram A - Straight Border

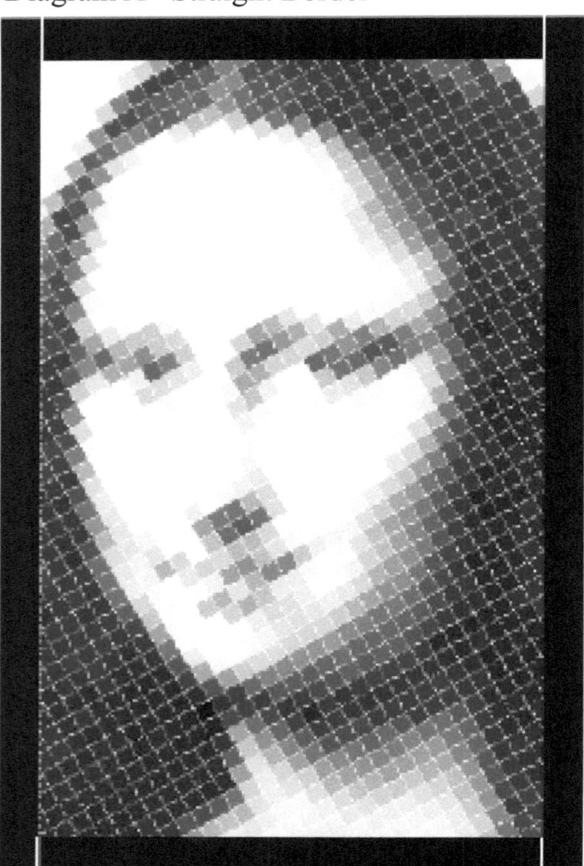

Diagram B - Mitered Border

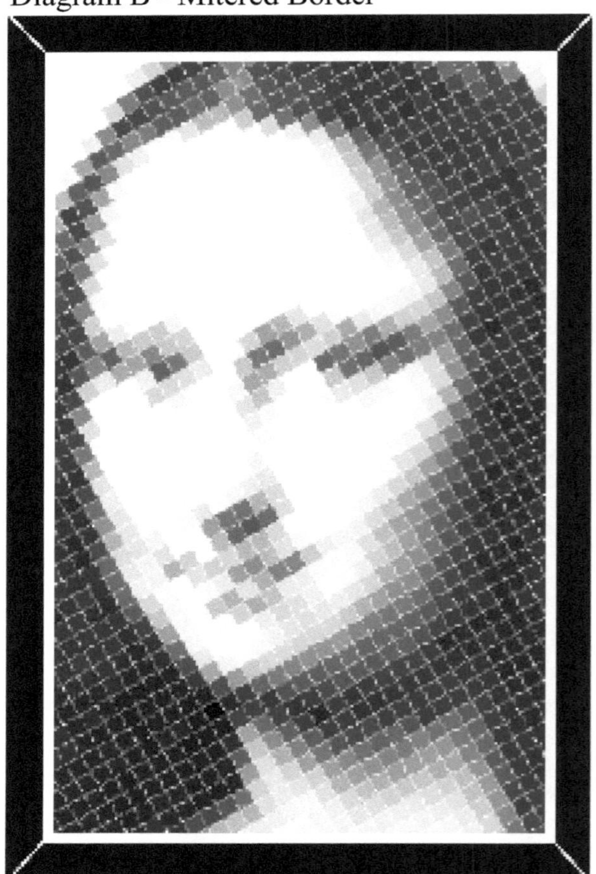

The center measurements will determine what length to cut the border strips. Cut the borders strips across the width of the border fabric.

Straight Border

A straight border has straight seams on the corners. See Diagram A on page 80. To add a straight border, the first step is to measure the center of the quilt horizontally. Cut two border strips this exact length. Stitch the borders to the sides of the quilt, easing the quilt top to match the border if it is necessary.

Next, measure the center of the quilt in the vertical direction including the border that you just applied. Cut two border strips that exact length. Stitch the border to the quilt, easing the two together if it is necessary. If you want a second straight border, repeat this process.

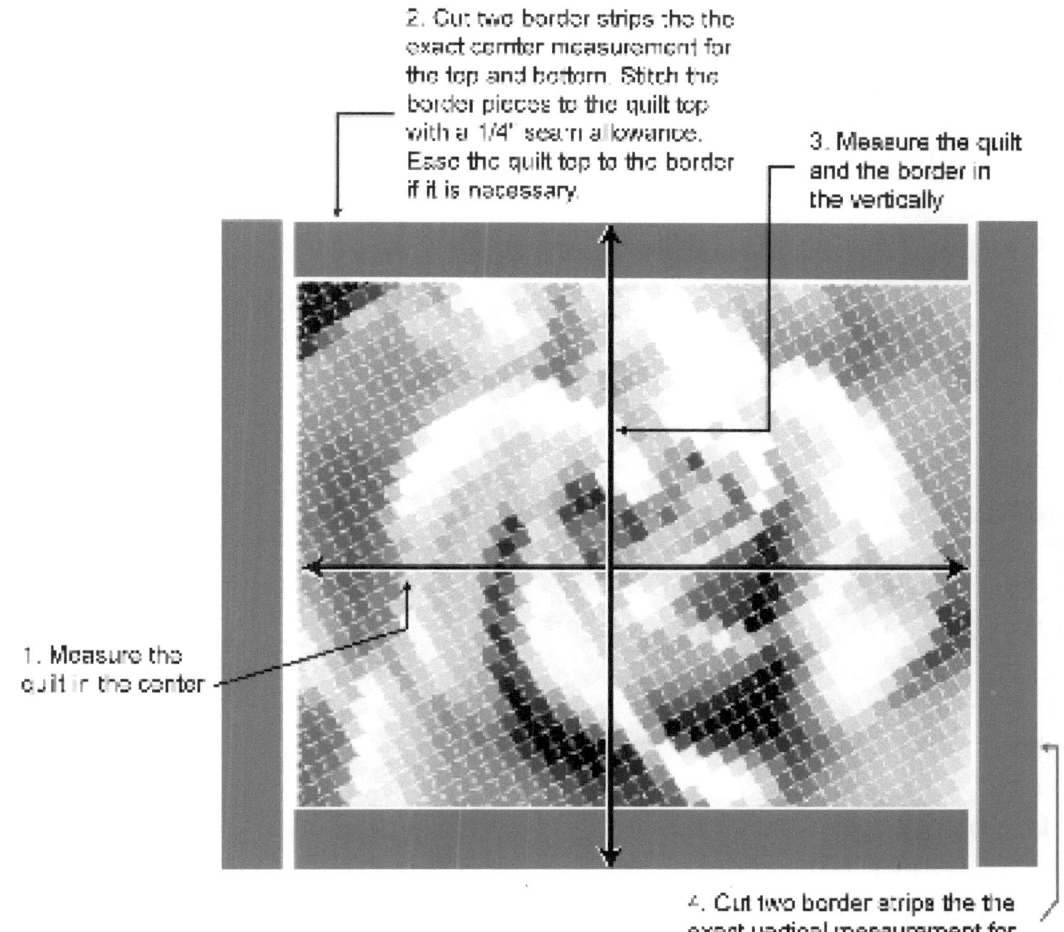

Create Mitered Corner

To make a mitered border (see diagram B on page 80), the strips of border fabric should be the center width measurement + two times the width of your border. Also measure the height of the quilt plus add two times the width of the border. You will need two of each size To sew the mitered corner, fold the quilt in half diagonally so that the ends of the border meet. Stitch the corner seams with 1/4" seam allowances. Repeat this step for all four corners.

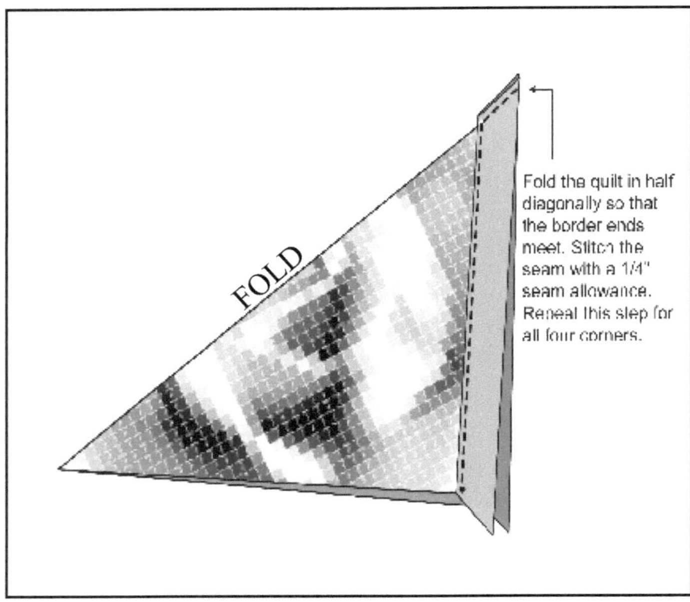

Batting And Backing

You can choose any backing fabric because the back of the quilt does not show. However I always use one of the fabrics that were used on the front of the quilt.

If your quilt top is larger than the width of the backing fabric, you will have to stitch two pieces of the backing fabric together to cover the back of the quilt. Remember to iron the backing seam open if a seam is required for your backing.

The batting you use between the quilt top and the backing is, again, a matter of your preference. Batting is sold in standard bedding sizes as well as by the yard. Cotton battings are flatter when they are finished than polyester battings, but polyester and cotton blends are a good option as well. I usually use 100% cotton batting for my quilts. You can find batting in fabric and quilt stores.

Basting

Basting is a temporary bond that holds the quilt top, batting and backing together. Basting also assures that you will not have tucks or folds on the backing when you stitch through your quilt sandwich.

You can baste the quilt sandwich by hand with a running stitch as shown in Exhibit B on page 83.

My favorite way to baste is to use an adhesive basting spray. Spray the adhesive between each layer of the quilt and the layers will hold together for the quilting process.

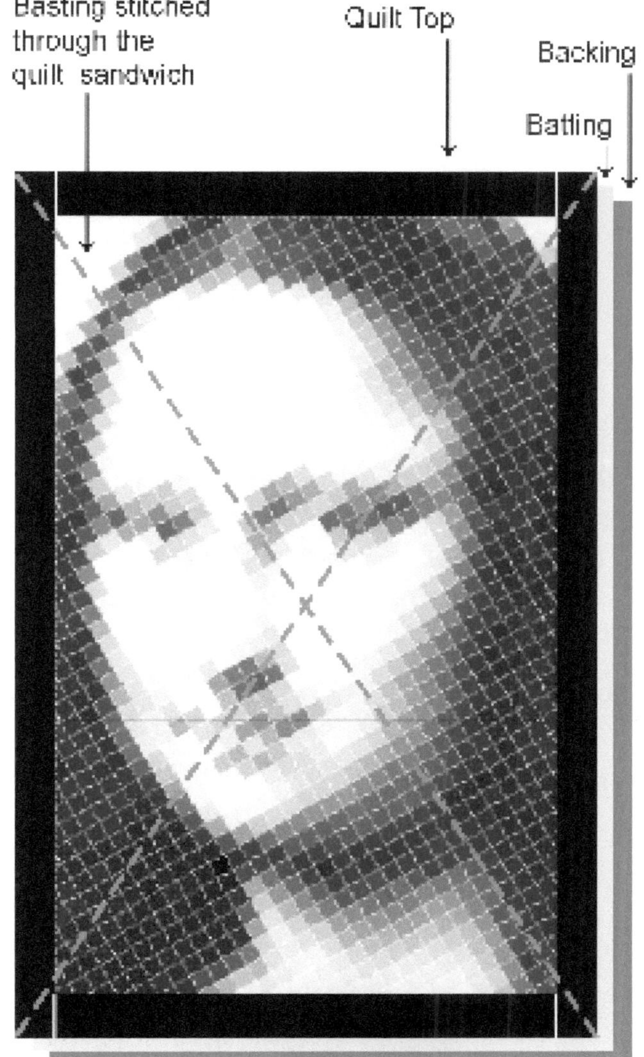

Exhibit B

Bindings

After the quilting is finished, you still need to finish the edges. You will finish the edges with a binding and I will show you how to make two different types. The first type of binding is a classic binding and the second type is an invisible binding.

Classic Binding

A classic binding will make a 1/4" edge around the outside of the quilt. To make a classic binding, the first thing you will do is cut strips 1 1/2" wide. Cut the strips across the width of the fabric. Stitch the strips together to form one long strip as shown below in Diagram A.

Diagram A

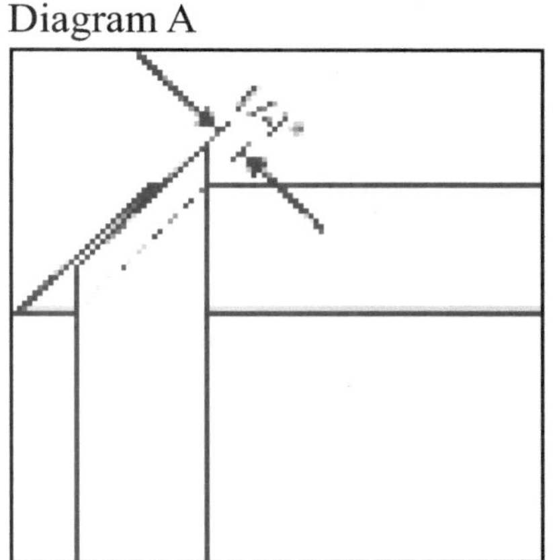

Fold the binding strip in half the long way, and then place the binding on the front of the quilt with the raw edges together. Stitch the binding with a ¼" seam allowance as shown in Diagram B.

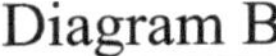
Diagram B

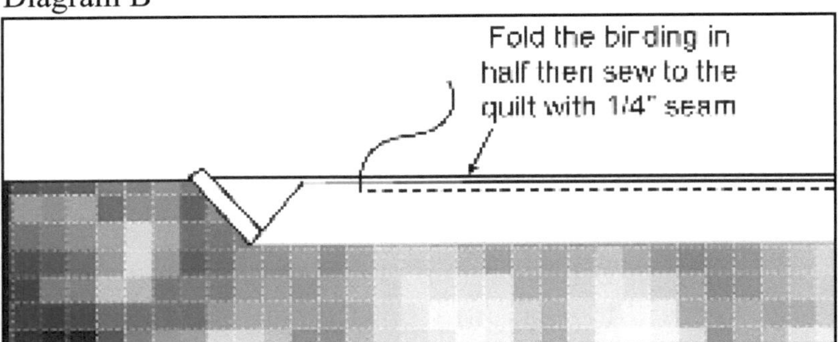

To continue the binding around the corner, stop stitching ¼" from the edge.

Diagram C

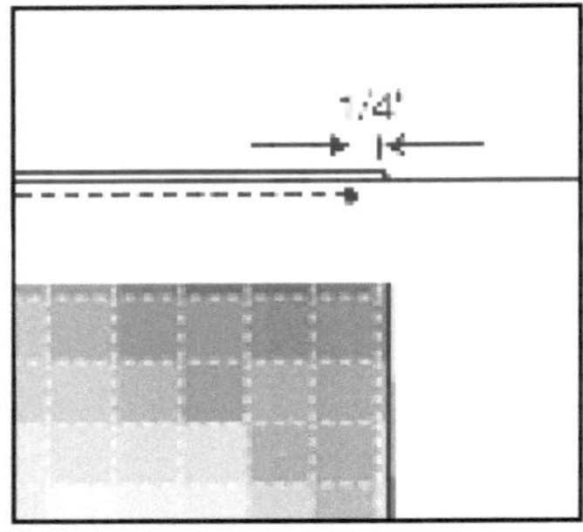

Fold the binding upward, creating an angled corner as shown in Diagram D.

Diagram D

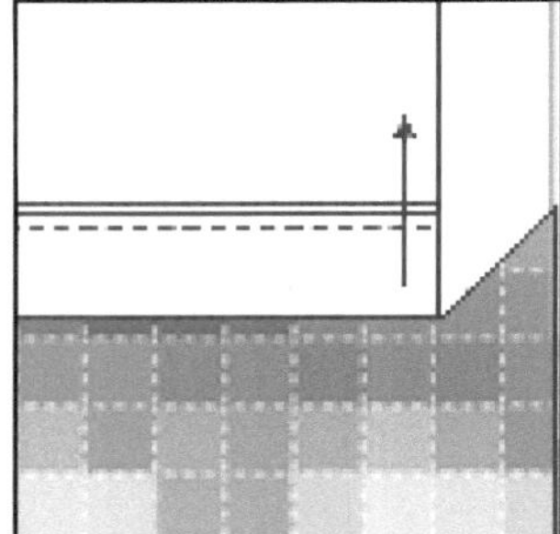

Then fold the binding back downward (creating a squared corner), leaving a fold of fabric as shown. Pin the fold in place and stitch the next side of the binding. You can begin stitching from the corner edge.

Diagram E

The next step is to wrap the binding around the quilt edge, then over to the back as shown in Diagram F. The last step is to stitch the edge of the binding in place by hand with a small whipstitch.

Diagram F

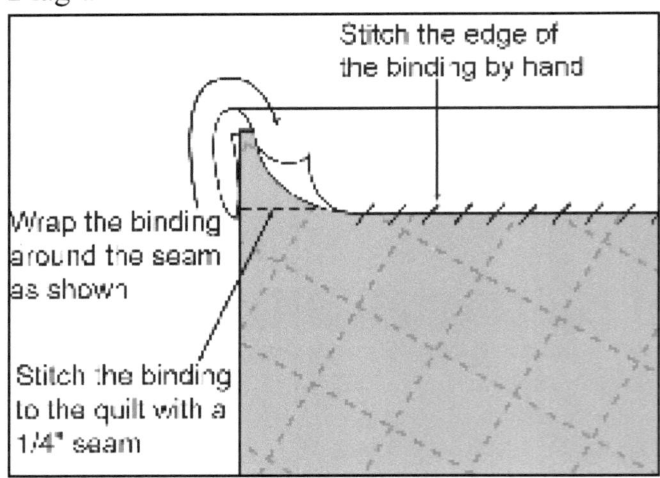

Invisible Binding

An invisible binding will not show at all when viewing the quilt from the front. To make an invisible binding, the first thing you will do is cut strips 1 1/2" wide. Fold the binding strip in half, and then place the binding on the front of the quilt with the raw edges together.

Stitch the binding with a 1/4" seam allowance as shown in Diagram B on page 84.

After stitching the binding all the way around the quilt, fold the binding and the seam upward, and away from the quilt. Stitch the binding 1/8" away from the seam as shown in the diagram below. This stitch will force the binding and the seam allowance to roll towards the back side of the quilt.

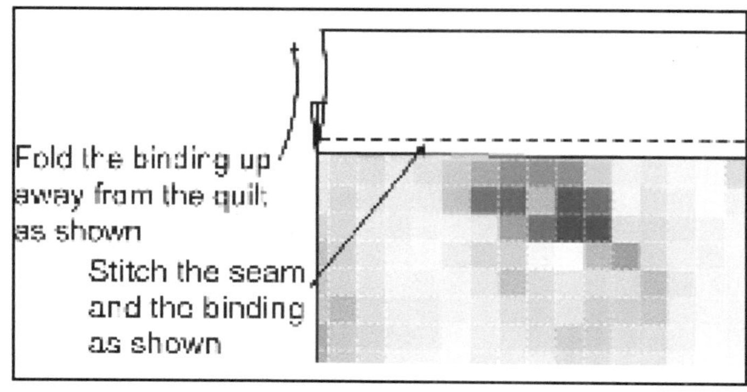

The last step is to stitch the edge of the binding in place by hand with a small whipstitch.

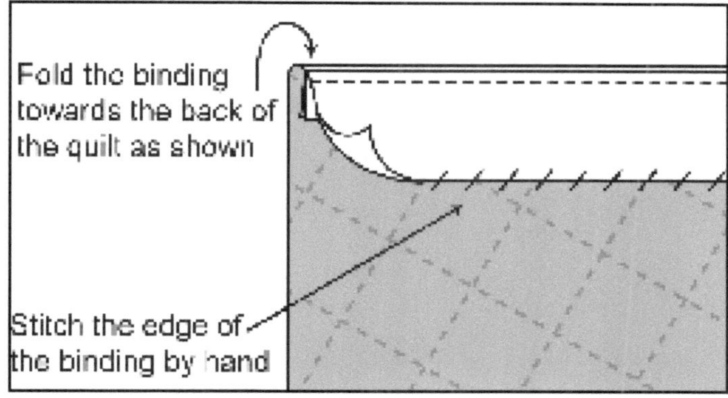

How To Display A Quilted Photo

When you prepare to display your quilt, you first need to think about how to care for the quilt. Since these quilts are intended to be art that is hung on a wall, you should not have to worry about the quilts getting dirty. However you will need to remove dust from time to time if they are not framed behind glass. To remove the dust, just put the quilt in a cool clothes dryer for 10 minutes. The dryer will remove the dust without damaging the quilt.

After you have learned how to care for your quilt, you must decide how you will display it. The most obvious way to display your quilt is to have it framed professionally.

Another way you can display the quilt is to stretch it over a blank canvas. If you want to stretch it on a canvas you will not need to add a backing, batting or a binding. Center it over the canvas, then use a staple gun to secure the quilt top to the wooden frame of the canvas.

The way that I prefer to display my quilts is to add a sleeve to the back of the quilt as shown in the diagram on the next page. To add a sleeve, just make a 4" fabric tube the width of the quilt, then hand stitch it to the top of the quilt on both sides of the tube. To hang the quilt you will need a cafe curtain rod. Apply the curtain rod to the wall according to the manufacturer's instructions. Pull the curtain rod through the sleeve to hang the quilt. You can buy cafe curtain rods at any hardware store.

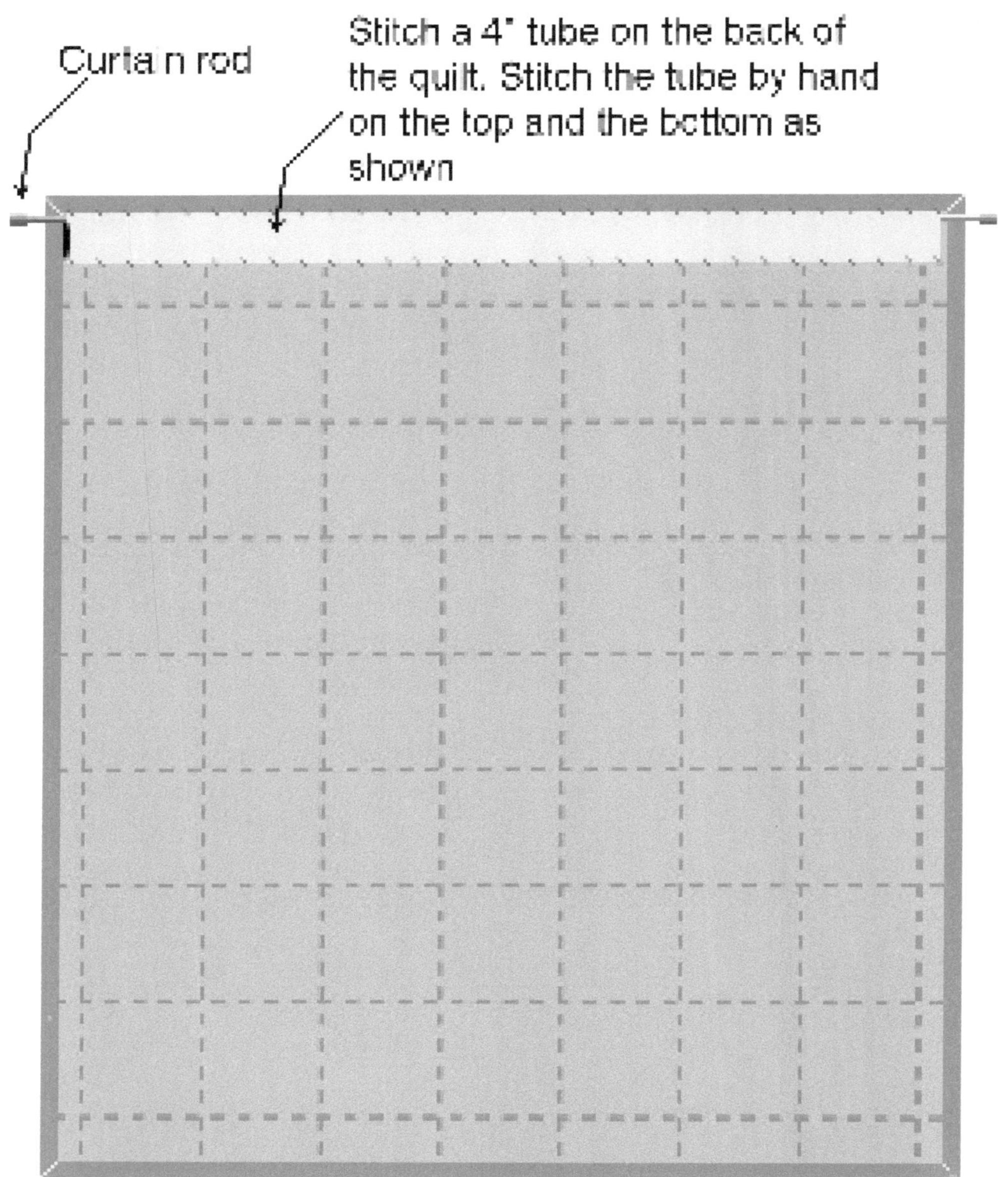
Curtain rod
Stitch a 4" tube on the back of the quilt. Stitch the tube by hand on the top and the bottom as shown

Summary Of Important Tips & Ideas

- Use 6 to 8 colors (or less) and your drawing will be easier to make! Page 15
- Use color wisely and choose the kind of impact you intend to make Page 16
- Avoid complicated pictures or pictures with many elements in them. Page 18
- Avoid pictures with many, many colors. If your picture has a complicated mix of colors, it will be difficult to choose so many fabrics that work well with one another. Page 19
- Remember FOCUS and LAYERS while planning your project. Page 31
- Select an assortment of fabrics of the same color for each color. Page 47
- Select one variegated thread for each color family used in the project. Page 48

New Ideas

#1 - Choose your artist. It can be your grandchild, it can be your child, it can be you, it can be anybody. Choose your artist.

#2 - Get your artist to draw you a picture. Get yourself to draw yourself a picture. It can be a house, it can be a car, it can be anything. Draw whatever you like, as long as you make it simple with just a few colors.

#3 - Make sure that you have only a few colors because we want simplicity. Simplicity doesn't mean it's going to be boring. Simplicity just means you have room to do amazing stitching and that is what makes it really amazing.

#4 - Follow the contours of the drawing or painting for the stitching!

#5 - When you look at a picture, imagine it as big wall art or as a giant art blanket!

Conclusion

My goal has been to teach you how to sew your own amazing stitched art from drawings or paintings. I hope you agree that I have reached my goal!

Will you share your success with me? I would like to see your quilts and I really want to hear your comments. To send your photos and comments, come visit me at: **www.HowToSewArt.com/success**

When you visit my website, please remember to register for your FREE Introductory webinar!

You will also get avideo course for free because you purchased this book. I will also send occasional emails to share my new techniques, offer exclusive student discounts, and I may even invite you to contribute to my next book! Register for your free bonus video course at: **www.HowToSewArt.com/sewart2class**

How To Claim Your Free Video Course

Several times in this book, I've promised to give you a free video course and a free trial of Quilted Photo Software. To keep my promise, I've prepared a registration page for you with all of the details.

Register for your free bonus video course and download software trial at this page: **www.HowToSewArt.com/sewart2class**

Thank you for your interest and I'll see you in the online class!

About The Author

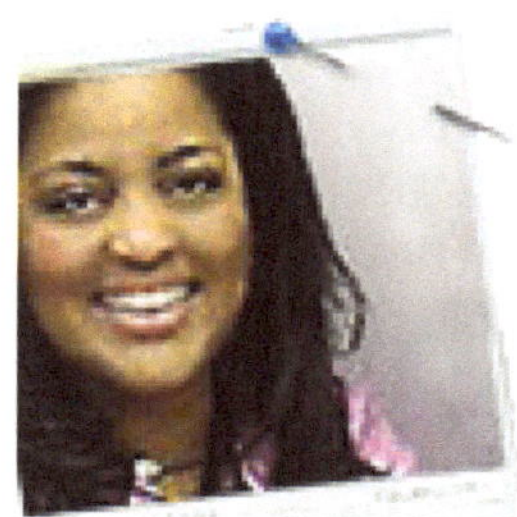

I began sewing at four years old. I made my own clothing in junior high and high school. I went on to fashion college (The Fashion Institute of Design and Merchandising). I studied fashion design, color theory and pattern making, and graduated in 1985. My 18 year fashion career included positions as a fashion designer, production patternmaker and a first patternmaker.

I remember watching "Quilt In A Day" with Eleanor Burns on PBS, but never tried to make one until I was at home after my daughter was born (Fall of 2000). I began to read books about quilting. I made my first quilt as a gift for my mother in November of 2000. I taught myself how to quilt by reading books, and watching the HGTV series, "Simply Quilts".

After making that first quilt, I wanted to design my own quilts. A few weeks later, I woke up with the beginnings of the ideas you learned in this book

I have been a guest on many popular quilting TV shows such as "Simply Quilts", "Kaye Wood and Friends" , "Sewing With Nancy" and look for me on Quilting Arts TV in Series 1500 and 1600.

I always knew that I would be an artist! I am also available to teach you how to be an artist too! Teaching classes and giving live lectures is the best part of my job! Please feel free to invite me to come see your group/guild. To find out about my availability, call 626-498-8234.

The Press...

"If you've looked at Tammie Bowser's amazing art quilts and thought, 'How does she do that?' or 'I could never make something so beautiful!' this book is your answer. Tammie breaks down her creative process and construction techniques into manageable bites, and explains it in simple language, so that anyone can learn it. Beyond the solid information and instructions, this book is an intimate look inside the mind and heart of a unique fiber artist with a great passion for teaching."

Susan Brubaker Knapp
Fiber artist, author, and host of Quilting Arts TV

"Tammie's quilted photos are so slick to make; they come together like magic! Besides being fun to make, It's fun to bask in all the compliments."

Ami Simms
Quilt book author, award winning quilter

"Tammie Bowser's methods give you the tools to make heirloom quality quilts on your first try. She has created a program that breaks down a process that would be unfathomably complicated for a busy quilter and makes it fun and fast to do. The results are nothing short of stunning in every case."

Sue Ann Taylor
Founder of Quilters News Network

"Your favorite photos recreated in fabric... what a fabulous idea! Tammie's easy to follow directions and her color value theories will help you preserve a memory in fabric"...

Kaye Wood
Television show host and author of 28 quilting books

How To Sew Art

You can make amazing quilted art easily when you know the secrets! Master the 9 secrets for transforming ordinary fabric into Fine Art! ...plus you'll get my Video Course for FREE ($47 value) as a bonus with book purchase!

Have you ever dreamed of being an artist? In this revolutionary new book, you will find the inspiring story of how Tammie Bowser became an artist and she'll teach you how to become an artist too. Tammie takes your hand and leads you step-by-step through the award winning Contoured Pixel Technique™. She uses this amazing technique to win art quilt contests and clients!

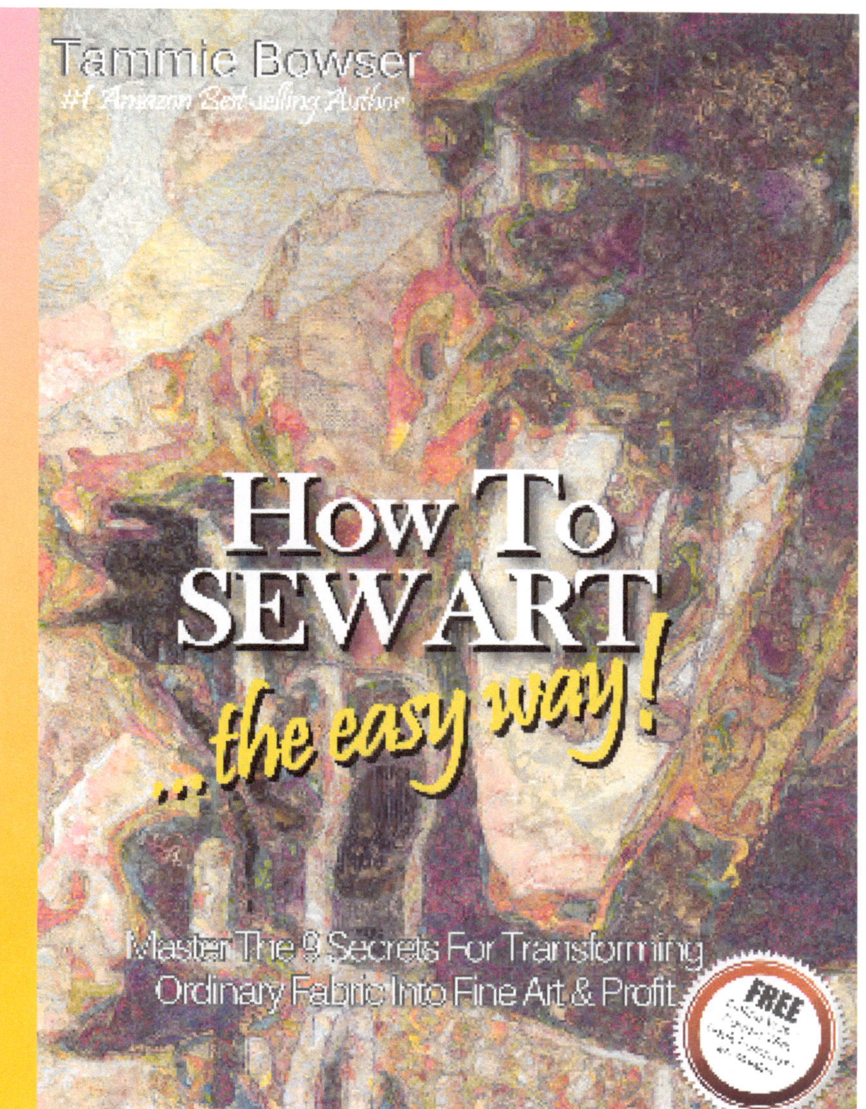

The Techniques Are Easy!
You will master the Core Concepts that make sewing art easy. Follow me and you'll be sewing fine art out of ordinary fabrics (available at any fabric store) and a sewing machine in as little as ONE WEEK! The diagrams and instructions make the process so easy to understand that even a beginner can do it! Each book comes with a free online video course to guide you.

Get This Book & Learn:

-How fabric can look like paint!

-To use thread like a paint brush!

-How to stitch the perfect image!

This book is a classic and a bestseller...it is a MUST HAVE! It is used as the textbook for the "How To Sew Art" home study course. Printed Books and Kindle Books are available.

Simply Amazing Quilted Photography

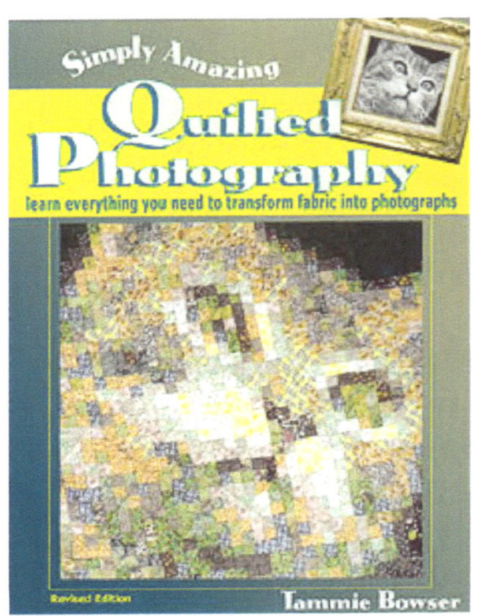

You can make amazing quilted art easily when you know the secrets! You'll learn all of the core concepts of Quilted Photography as well as how to choose fabric and even how the pick the best photos. This book is a classic and a bestseller...it is a MUST HAVE! It is used as the textbook for the "Simply Amazing Quilted Photography" home study course. Printed Books and Kindle Books are available.

More Amazing Quilted Photography

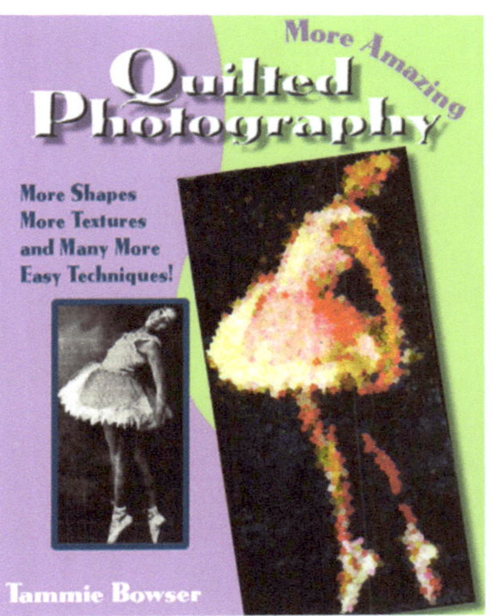

You can make amazing quilted art easily when you know the secrets! The ballerina quilt on the cover was purchased by Shelburne Museum in Vermont and Tammie will teach you exactly how to make it in this book! You'll learn how to make pixel quilts that look less digital and more painted! We'll explore raw edge applique' and freemotion quilting. This book is a MUST HAVE! It is used as the text book for the More Amazing Quilted Photography home study course. Printed Books and Kindle Books are available.

Amazing Chenilled Quilted Photography

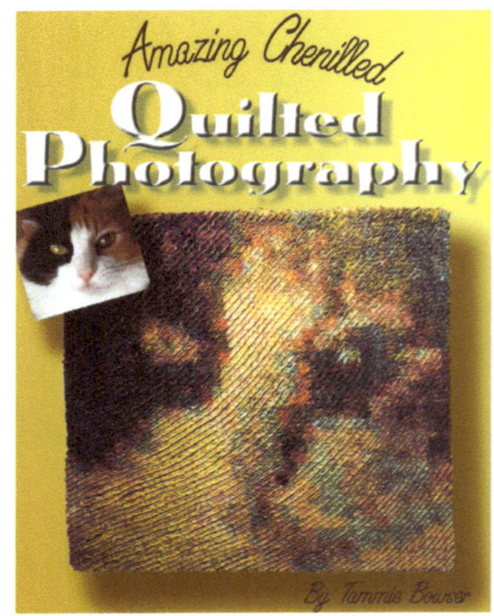

You can make amazing quilted art easily when you know the secrets! You'll learn how to make photo quilts with texture! This book will teach you how to make amazing furry animal quilts and more. If you have any of the other Quilted Photography books, then this book will be an amazing addition to your collection. Printed Books and Kindle Books are available.

Quilted Photo Deluxe 2.0

Want advanced Art Quilt features? Well here it is! You can make the kind of quilts you learned about in this book, and you can make all of the styles of patterns from all of my books! Quilted Photo Deluxe 2.0 has 16 pixel shapes, basic square pixel patterns, paper piecing patterns and you can automatically design the award winning Contoured Pixel patterns! This is the technique I used to design my award winning art quilts! Quilted Photo Deluxe 2.0 is the best art quilt software in the world. It is easy to use and reliable. This program is part of a family of software programs created especially for art quilts.

It includes options for grayscale or realistic color palettes. You can also print a shopping design sheet that tells you how much of each fabric you will need, finished quilt dimensions and more. The most time saving feature is the full-size printing feature! Quilted Photo Deluxe 2.0 also contains all of the functions of my "Valuations" software at no extra charge! Just tape the pattern pages together, and you will be ready to start!

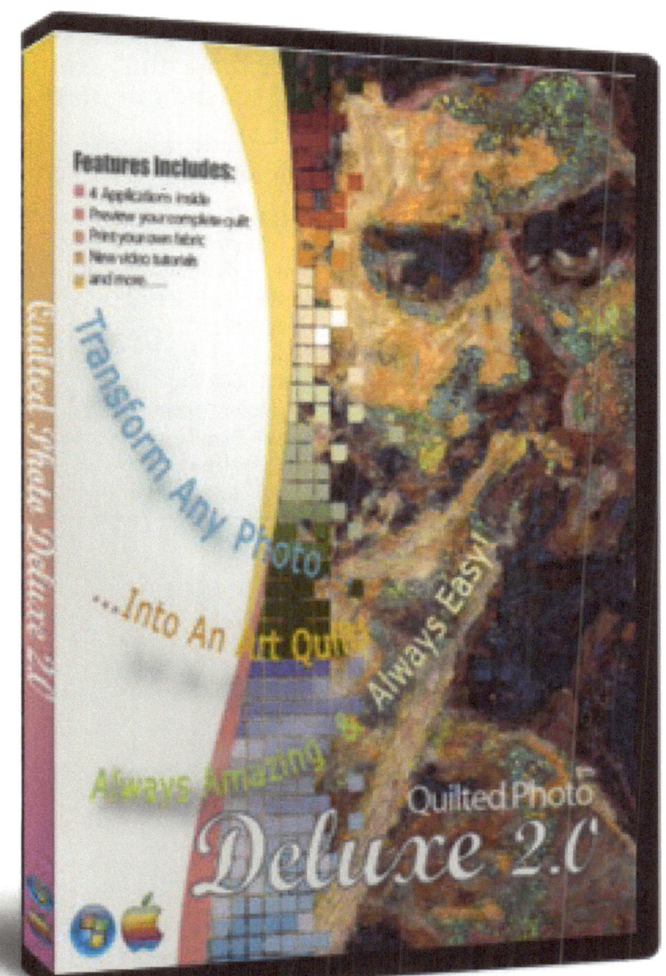

Video Demo at:
www.HowToSewArt.com/Demo

Features & Benefits Of QPD 2.0

·Easily adjust the Contrast or Brightness of your photo! Your photos don't have to be perfect, just fix it with QPD 2.0!

·You get more design options... Grayscale, Realistic, and you can even use the built in fabric collections!

·You have full control of the number of squares and the number of fabrics!

·You get complete control of the finished dimensions of the quilt. So now you can easily design an art quilt that is the perfect size to fit your wall!

·You can see a preview of the pattern before you print it out! The patterns now have large numbers!!!

·The palette has large color swatches! Print it out to match your fabrics!

·You can also import your own fabrics into the preview and see your quilt before you cut even one fabric!!

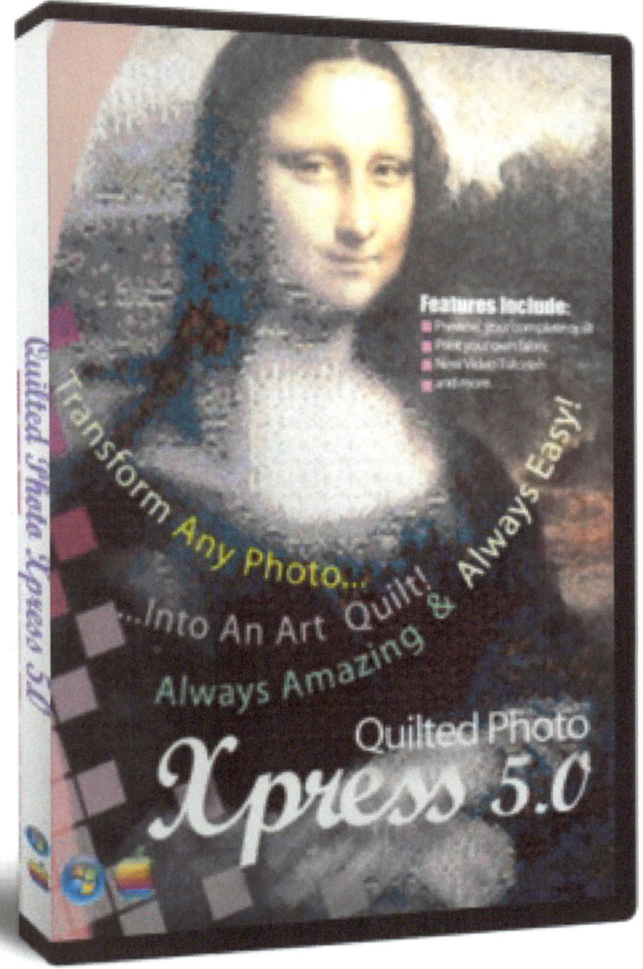

Quilted Photo Xpress 5.0

Do you want basic and economical art quilt software? Then Quilted Photo Xpress 5.0 is what you need. This program is part of a family of software programs created especially for art quilting. This software makes classic pixel patterns as well as the Kids Drawing Patterns you learned about in this book without all of the extra bells and whistles. Quilted Photo Xpress 5.0 is our simple and streamlined quilting software.

The QPX5.0 software includes design options for grayscale or realistic fabric palettes. You can also print a shopping design sheet that tells you how much of each material you will need, finished quilt size and more. The most exciting and time saving new feature is the full-size printing feature! You can print your patterns with your numbers (or colors) inside the squares! Just tape the patterns pages together, and you will be ready to start!

All software available for Windows and MAC

Windows Requirements
Pentium III 500MHz
512MB Ram (recommended)
20MB free HD Space
32MB VRAM video card
Windows 98/ME/XP/2000/Vista
Windows 7, 8 and 10

Mac Requirements
Recommended Systems:
-Mac Mini (Intel Based Only)
-iMac (Intel Based Only)
-Macbook
-Macbook Air
-Macbook Pro
Complete Specifications:
-1GB Ram (recommended)
-20MB free Harddrive Space
-10.5 (Leopard) to 10.14 (Mojave)

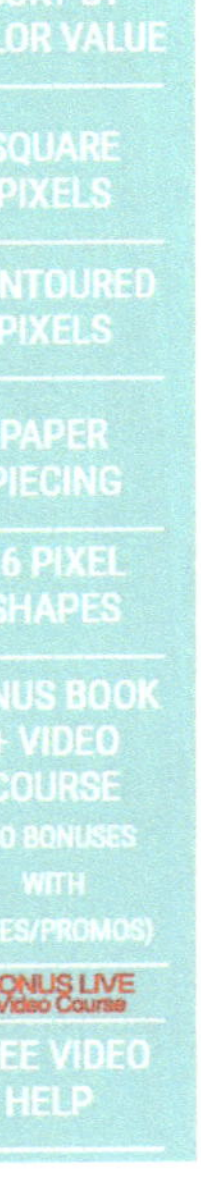

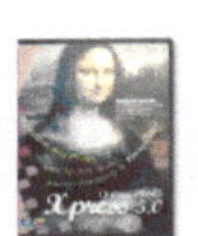

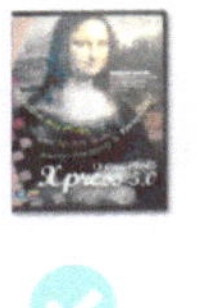

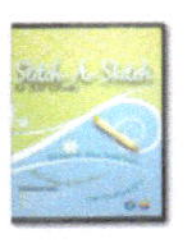

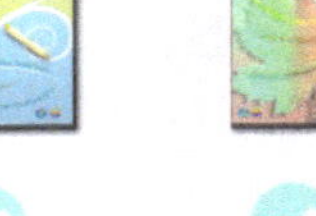

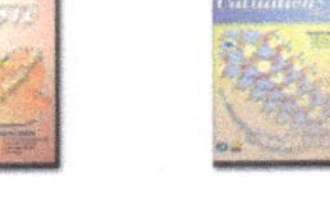

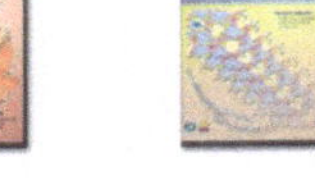

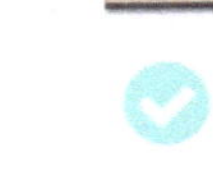

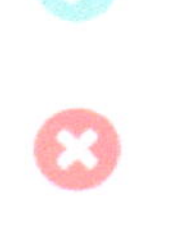

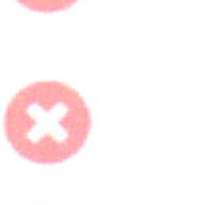

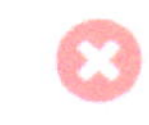

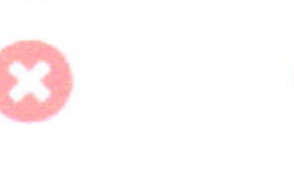

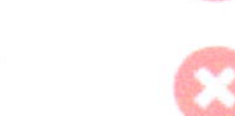

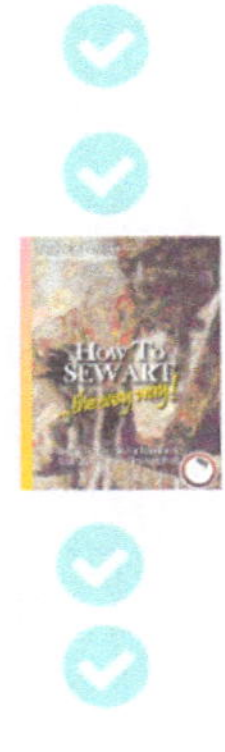

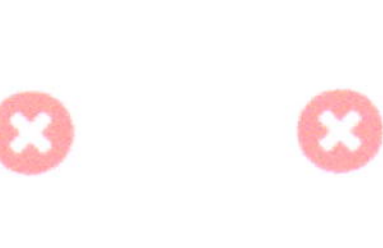

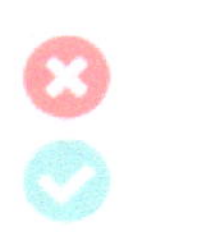

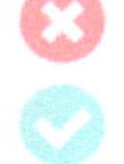

	BEST DEAL				
SORT BY COLOR VALUE	✓	✓	✓	✓	✓
SQUARE PIXELS	✓	✓	✗	✗	✗
CONTOURED PIXELS	✓	✗	✓	✗	✗
PAPER PIECING	✓	✗	✗	✓	✗
16 PIXEL SHAPES	✓	✗	✗	✗	✗
BONUS BOOK + VIDEO COURSE (NO BONUSES WITH SALES/PROMOS)		✗	✗	✗	✗
New! BONUS LIVE Video Course	✓	✗	✗	✗	✗
FREE VIDEO HELP	✓	✓	✓	✓	✓
	$249.95	$99.95	$99.95	$99.95	$39.95

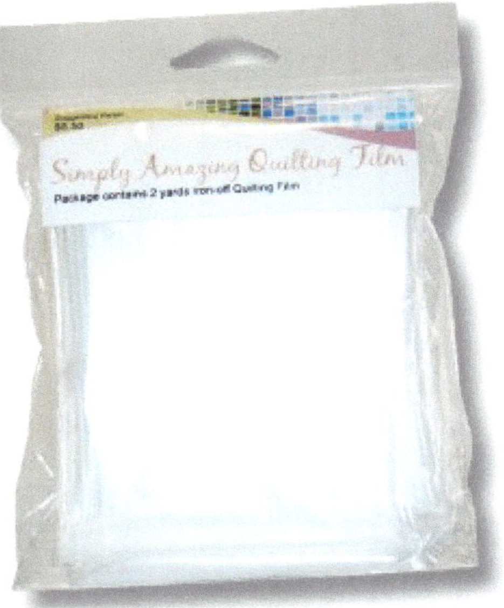

Amazing Quilting Film

This package contains 2 yards of iron-off quilting film. This inexpensive film is a priceless aid for easy free motion quilting. It is visually clear, so you can see right through it! This quilting film is 40" wide. Use with 100% cotton fabric only.

Extra – Wide Fusible Tricot

This fusible interfacing was carefully tested for use with Quilted Photography projects. It is transparent, lightweight, and has a superior adhesive to firmly hold the fabric pieces in place. This tricot is so thin that your finished quilt will remain super soft. The interfacing is 60" wide and the package contains 2 yards. Imported from France.

Extra – Wide Fusible Web

This fusible webbing was carefully tested for use with Quilted Photography projects. It is transparent, lightweight, and has a superior adhesive to firmly hold the fabric swatches in place. This fusible web is a must have if you are making your own home made "Sticky Web" (See page 46). Three times wider than any fusible web you can get in retail fabric stores. This fusible web is 60" wide! The package contains 2 yards.

New From Mosaic Quilt Studio

"LIVE" Interactive Zoom Classes

It would be my pleasure to teach you face to face!

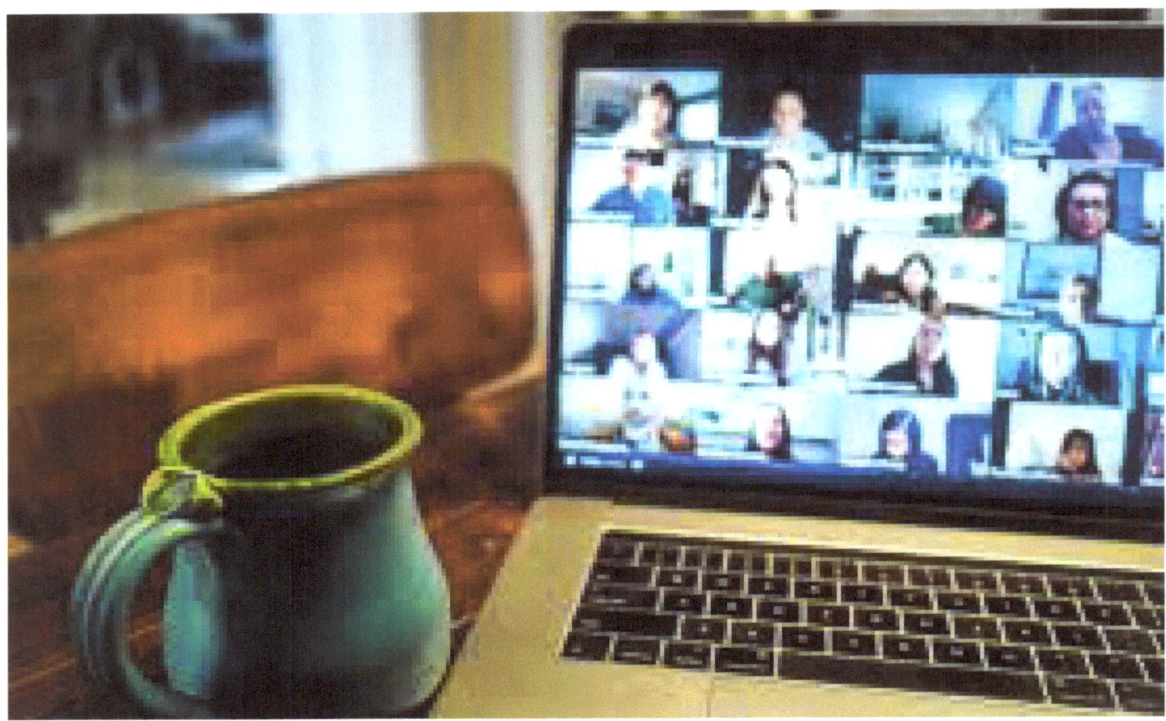

Visit the HowToSewArt.com to register!

Simple and Amazing Strip Technique Class:

Learn to transform ordinary fabric strips into unbelievably beautiful photographic quilts! The quilts look intricate and difficult to make, but it's easy…even if you are just beginning to quilt. Each quilted photo takes only a few hours to make and you'll learn the simple techniques that will guarantee your success. Your friends will be amazed when they realize your quilt is really a photograph! Class includes a custom pattern made from your photo.

Contoured Technique Class:

Ever dream of being a real artist? Find out the simple, step by-step creative process of transforming ordinary fabrics from any fabric store into fine art! Learn how to easily make fabric look like paint and how to use thread like a paint brush. Even beginners can sew perfect quilted art!

We will use organic, free form shapes. This class is the next step after the "Simple and Amazing Strip Technique " class. We will explore new ideas and techniques for using ordinary fabrics and thread. Your quilt will look like a stunning painting…. no paint needed! You'll make a portrait from your own photo for this class.

Always Amazing & Always Easy!

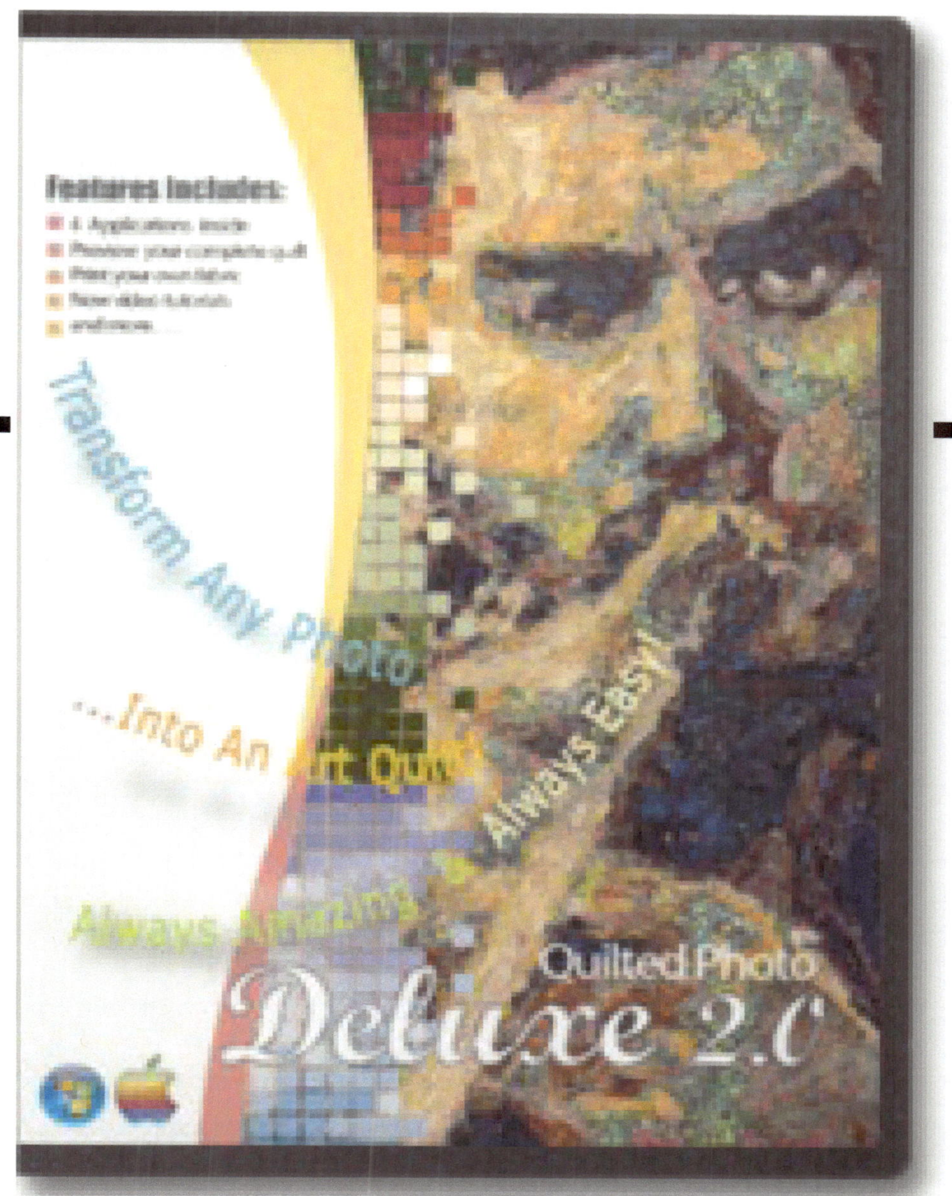

SAVE $50 OFF

Quilted Photo Deluxe

Coupon Code: 50offhtsa2

Visit the HowToSewArt.com to redeem coupon

Notes

Notes

www.ingramcontent.com/pod-product-compliance
Lightning Source LLC
LaVergne TN
LVHW070216110826
845147LV00003B/586
* 9 7 8 1 8 8 7 4 6 7 0 4 9 *